the times of
MY LIFE

DR MARIE WEIR

Typeset in New Century Schoolbook LT Std

Design, typesetting, editing and publishing by UK Book Publishing

UK Book Publishing is a trading name of Consilience Media

www.ukbookpublishing.com

ISBN: 978-1-910223-61-1

The times of my life: Acknowledgements

My life has been a joy with a new challenge presenting itself every ten years or so. My challenges and opportunities have been set against a background of huge social, health, economic and educational change from the 1920s through the depression of the 1930s, WWII, the birth of the National Health Service and the impact of the application of behavioural psychologies.

For me personally the most challenging ten years have been the most recent. I have recovered from a severe attack of osteoporosis and a stroke which has left me partially sighted. Whilst I have been able to handwrite my story I have been unable to read what I have written so I have many people to thank for making this book possible.

It is difficult to thank all of them but I would like to mention a few.

I would like to express my particular thanks to my daughters *Sally*, for being my editor in chief and 'on tap' consultant, and *Shona*, for ensuring that my handwritten manuscript was photocopied and sent to *Rosanne Houston* for typing.

All my family have been a constant support to me. Their patience, loving interest and encouragement have been unfailing.

Rosanne did a magnificent job in deciphering and converting my hand written text to print thus giving first life to the book.

I also thank *Joyce Cunningham* for her enthusiastic encouragements and for putting me in touch with *UK Book Publishing Ltd*. *Ruth Lunn* and the *UK Book Publishing* team have been most helpful and supportive in helping us to find the best narrative perspective because the book was originally written in the third person, and in ensuring a professional publication. Some names have been changed to protect anonymity.

Other publications by Dr Marie Weir

- *Women's Hockey For the '70s:*
  ISBN 0 7182 0978 8: Kaye & Ward 1974

- *Hockey Coaching A Psychological Approach to the Women's*
  Game: ISBN 0 7182 1113 8: Kaye & Ward 1977

- *Ferries in Scotland: ISBN 0 85976 235 1:*
  John Donald Publishers LTD 1988

Dedication

I dedicate this book to all the significant people in my 90 years of living, especially to my *Mum* and *Dad*, *Auntie Nan* and *the family*, with my ever constant thanks for their loving support.

Chapter 1

*A*n ordinary, unremarkable girl – that's me! Why then am I trying to write a book? Heaven knows if anyone will ever read it. I would if I were a reader. To me it is interesting, informative and worth the time spent in trying to fit an individual life into the huge social changes that have taken place practically daily throughout the almost 90 years of my existence.

God must be constantly entertained as he has a grand-stand view of the world as it twists and turns between good and bad.

As for me the desire to put pen on to paper (now lap-top!) was in my genes, inherited I think from my ancestor Angus Black, a renowned author of his day. So, here goes! It must be fulfilled – now!

And you, dear reader, are the target. My hope is that as friends you and I can enjoy some of the stories and events as they occur, even though they may be from an ordinary girl.

The first thing that happened was that I was born.

How good, or otherwise, that was for my mother I'm not sure. It happened on a farm, Chapelbank, Perthshire. I was on time, I believe, but the local nurse delivered me with dirty fingernails – no antibiotics in those days!

My mother, Lilias (Lily), took time to recover to enjoy the joys of a first baby, but the weather was a summery June 1926. Mum, a trained PE teacher, was a devotee of fresh air and this baby was wrapped up, put in the pram and pushed into the garden for the good of her health.

The arrival of this much wanted baby fitted neatly into the farm's pattern of growth development and rest. It was this atmosphere that embraced the newcomer into the happy, apparently carefree parents' lifestyle and I flourished under the guard of Dad's aging sheepdog Don.

The farm house was Mum's base. It was set in the midst of flat, fertile fields. Friday was traditionally market day in Perth. The following day, Saturday, was the best day of the week. It was cricket's day. Come rain or shine nothing changed the importance of Saturday, week by week. Dad was fully committed from the moment he leapt out of bed at 6am on Saturday mornings.

He could not get essential jobs on the farm done quickly enough. Freedom! Cricket beckoned. Home games on the North Inch or away to Aberdeen, Forfar or Fife. For Dad the adrenalin rush of one-day cricket, knocking up 100 runs, stumping a wicket – or two or three – and a write up in the Perthshire Advertiser with the Scottish selectors scrutinising potential internationalists were the stuff of life. All these elements and more mixed to provide excitement for often up to 10,000 spectators. His wicket-keeping skills were much admired and he was renowned as a safe pair of hands. Even more, Dad's batting was aggressive and yet reliable; he was the match winner on many occasions.

All through her baby years, I absorbed the atmosphere and I adopted Saturday as my special day of the week too.

My mother, although a PE teacher, was a dancer, not a games player, but soon complemented the games enthusiasms of her husband with her social charm. Lily was attractive and immediately found her place in the hierarchy of the ladies' influential circle in Perth. Every Friday and Saturday she accompanied the wives of the other important men for afternoon tea.

For Mum within these connections, there was order and safety.

At home Mum supervised staff help. They were well trained and made life comfortable and easy. There was the cook, Agnes. She provided good solid Scottish fare. She, together with Meggie the Nursery maid, ensured that I thrived.

My grandparents, Mum's mother and father, brothers and sister, and cousins, the Walkers all lived and worked in Bathgate. So Mum's achievement of buying a new car was special.

For my first ride I was wrapped up in a thick shawl, a woollen hat and leggings. Mum snuggled into a fur coat – her feet in a sheep-skin rug, her head in a fur-lined leather hat. Dad braved the elements in a leather jacket and plus fours. They were all equipped to face any weather.

The car was a T-Ford, with a roof that could be wound open or shut. It was a beautiful day, cold but sunny.

I slept all the way.

That journey between Chapelbank and Bathgate set the foundation for many a happy hour. The car was a wonderful place. I could fall into a deep sleep and dream impossible dreams. Or, I would gaze at the passing countryside and imagine the views from the high hills.

At the end of the journey I always had my own personal welcoming committee. I took it all for granted as my right.

I was always aware of being the privileged granddaughter. I responded accordingly. It suited me to recognise that I was 'Granny's best girl', even although Granny protested loudly that she never had any favourites.

The adults kissed and cuddled me, glad to see each other and delighted to admire the baby.

'Beautiful!' 'Such a good weight!' 'Fair like her mother!' 'Like her grandmother too!' And on they went.

Why do people feel it necessary to drool over new babies, and hand them around?

As a baby I believe I was not too unattractive. My looks would certainly have been enhanced by the long cotton and lace dress my mother had bought. She had bought it in McEwans of Perth. This was one of the most popular dress shops in Scotland. It was on a level with Jenners and Darlings in Edinburgh.

Mum had impeccable taste and dressed herself and her daughter in the most fashionable clothes.

McEwans of Perth was Mum's favourite shop. She knew it well but came to know it even better after marriage to Joe. She discovered that one of Dad's brothers, Bob, had trained in McEwans as an expert in 'lingerie'. He subsequently left Perth to be employed at Liberty's in London. There, he was so successful that he became appointed chief advisor in Liberty's to Queen Mary.

This was about the same time that his niece was born. As a present, he sent me an up-to-date pink cot blanket which covered me on the journey home to Chapelbank. The car travelled at 25 mph, and the journey home was tedious. However, Meggie, the little nursery maid, and Agnes, the cook-general, were waiting at Chapelbank to welcome the family home.

Shortly after this the Smith world would begin to change. For a time agriculture was an essential part of the 1914-18War as it fed the nation.

Mum found Dad more than once standing in front of a framed letter hanging in his office. She knew what it said as well as he did. They had often read it together.

She slipped her hand into his. "You did well during the war," she told him. "The nation depended on you men to keep us from starvation! Signed by Lloyd George." She read that part aloud.

"That was all very well then but we have to survive now. That is a bit more difficult."

He turned towards her to kiss her lovingly.

"It seems we're doing alright."

"If all our buyers of beasts and pigs were as generous as your brother Johnny, I wouldn't need to worry!"

"It's the way the family have been brought up!" Lily swung on Joe's arm.

"Careful," he cautioned. "You nearly knocked out my cigarette."

"Sorry!" Lily drew back and bent to kiss her husband again.

The nurse maid brought me in to say 'Good-night' to my parents. It had been an adventurous day.

Chapter 2

At just three years old I glanced wonderingly down the long, straight driveway that led to Chapelbank Farm's front door. My father drove slowly as the house receded; he could not bear to follow my gaze as it was too painful.

This would be the last time he would take the car down the drive as owner of the farm.

Sitting in the front seat, tears trickled down Mum's cheeks. She had always thought her life would be spent at Chapelbank. After all, Joe had been living there long before she had met him. There had been no sign of any financial difficulties until that awful letter arrived from "old man" Smith – Joe's father.

I was blissfully unaware of my parents' financial problems. I only knew that very little had changed in my small world except I had a new cot.

This larger, blue painted fold-up cot was solemnly erected outside the front door in the warm summer sunshine. From this vantage point I was able to monitor all the farm yard's comings and goings.

Then suddenly, there had been a change. Mum and Dad seemed upset and did not smile or laugh in ways they had done before.

It was not long before I watched as all my toys were being packed into boxes.

It all came together on this day in the car with the hard core of my life being changed;

Joe was well known and well liked in Perth. Similarly, Lily could depend on the Walker family in Bathgate. Until now time had passed pleasantly enough. I established my own group of friends. I loved going out and about. The outstanding social activities were the parties held at Windsor Rooms in Perth. They were fabulous especially when the mum who was the hostess knew how to run them. Otherwise they could end up in utter chaos. Mum was great, she kept good discipline but it was still fun.

The best activity, especially for the boys, was the slippery, polished wood floor. I would lead the queue at the top of the run in. I was not so particular about causing damage to my pretty party dress. Competing with the boys was the thing! The other mothers watched with various degrees of disapproval clear on their faces.

But now something terrible was happening. Even I, aged three, knew it was serious.

Dad had been breeding a herd of beef cattle. They had been doing pretty well in the Perth and Stirling markets.

Occasionally he had been tempted to buy a few Highland cattle 'on the hoof'. They had trekked from the Isle of Kerrera so were thin and tired. Joe thought he could build them up and sell them at a profit. It would be a nice little extra bonus and he had done it before.

The day after Dad had bought the cattle the family drove passed the field they were in, on their way to Bathgate.

"Looking good!" he remarked to Lily.

"They should sell well at Perth next Friday. We could go for high tea. Would you like to do that? Bet Marie would, wouldn't you?" Joe turned his head towards the back seat.

I agreed loudly and climbed into the front seat to land between my parents. No such things as seat belts then. Everyone just rattled around in the car.

On the way home from Bathgate the enormity of the disaster did not fully strike Dad as he drove slowly between the fields where the Highland cattle had been released. Mum sat still in the car. Dad pushed himself out and stood and stared. I was uncertain what to do. In the silence of my parents I sensed something was badly wrong. If I could've reached my thumb to suck I would have sucked it. As it was my bottom lip trembled and quietly I cried.

The new cattle seemed to be frothing at the mouth. There was an eerie silence.

Lily caught sight of John Rugg, the cattleman, walking on the far side of the field. He was going from beast to beast to judge their state of health.

These were all the things I can clearly remember of that terrible day.

Soon, my memory of the cattle fadedyet the whole issue arose again when I was told we were all going to move to another farm. The cattle had foot and mouth disease and all my father's cattle had to be destroyed. Although Dad had successfully managed the farm for ten years his father sold the farm and evicted his son. This must have been devastating for Dad and Mum as they started to look for a new job and a new future. Through Dad's farming contacts he was recommended for the job of Estate and Farm Manager for Mr McAndrew who had newly acquired a local estate. But I knew nothing of this sitting in the back of the car that day.

Chapter 3

My introduction to the estate began with a low key ride into an immaculate steading. On the way into this steading I was captivated by a large mirror giving improved sight on a 'hidden' corner in the village of Comrie. It was placed on the wall of the of the estate factor's office. It was the first of the five star additional extras that Mr McAndrew, the owner of the estate, perceived as essential.

Of course the mirror and its positioning were great assets for better safety on the corner. On first encounter I was taken with the size of it and thought it was a remarkable thing. Surely all mirrors were small, round, and hand-held. Mum's mirror was silver and rested on her dressing table. It was used to examine the blemishes on a face. At least that was how Mum used it.

As my father parked in front of the Manager's stately Victorian mansion I rushed excitedly into the front door entrance. There I bumped into Nettie.

Nettie was the new cook-general who had come from the kitchen to greet her new employers. She was a lovely person and a reliable cook of good straight-forward Scottish fare. Nothing too fancy but things like 'real' Scottish porridge with salt – not sugar, although for Joe she made an exception! Later he became an expert porridge maker himself! I wanted to follow his example but was strictly held to the

'No sugar in porridge rule'!

Mum held out her hand to me and together we entered the kitchen which had a stone floor and a big range for all the cooking. Nettie looked in complete control of her domain but I could spot a smaller, younger girl lurking in the shadows. My mother noticed this figure too.

"Come out, Lizzie," she said kindly. "Come and meet Marie." But I turned shy too and the pair of us stayed put.

I studied the nurse maid – because that was her role. Little did I know then that Lizzie was to play such a big part in my life over the next ten years. At that first meeting I was more intrigued by seeing all over the house. My mother was curious too.

Lily took her husband's arm.

"Joe, let's have a walk around outside. I want to see the whole place."

"Yes, we can do that although I wonder what Nettie has got prepared for us. It smells very nice." He smiled across at the older woman – he was renowned for his warm smile. He also had a great deal of practice in dealing with cook-generals. After all he had been looked after by one at Chapelbank as a bachelor for ten years.

Nettie unfolded her arms.

"I have your supper for later on," she said. "I thought you would be tired after your long drive."

The farm buildings were made of old grey stones. The modernised steading had a granary which ran the length of it. Behind the steading was a cluster of buildings. These housed several byres where different varieties of cattle munched their afternoon feed. There were a number of Aberdeen Angus cows in calf next to a restless beast of a bull. Everything was neat and well maintained; several men were busily removing manure and sweeping up the debris. They all bobbed their heads in Dad's direction as he made his inspection. They were curious to see what the new man looked like.

I wanted to push ahead. I wanted to see the stable and the horses. Dad persisted in taking what was known as the scenic route. This way led via the hen house and the yard where the bales of hay were stacked.

Finally, we entered the stables with stalls down both interior walls for twelve big Clydesdale horses. The building was impressive both inside and out. Each stall housed a single horse. Its tack, consisting of big, shining polished leather, was stored on the side of the dividing partition constructed of best pine wood with brass handles and knobs decorating it.

The horses shifted peacefully from one foot to the other. And little notices headed the narrow wall at the end of each stall. In clear print the name of each horse was written.

The smell of horses was strong – penetrating. I loved it.

"Can we go and pat the horses?" I asked. Queenie was my own little Shetland pony that Dad had transported to the new Estate from Chapelbank for me to ride. We found Queenie comfortably settled with her head stuck into a bucket of food and a soft bed of straw awaiting her.

Dad led us back to the kitchen and took me into the large, rather imposing lounge. Mum looked round. What she saw did not please her. "I think we have to get some new furniture," she said to Dad. "It's a good thing we were given so many good wedding presents," she added.

"I'm sure you'll manage as you always do, my darling," Dad replied.

Subsequently, I accompanied my mother to Love's, the auctioneer, an exclusive furniture shop in Perth. We bought a three piece suite that improved the seating space and added fashionable furnishings, thus turning the room into an up-to-date 1920s' style.

The rhythm of the farm was soon established and I quietly made up my play patterns. The big branched tree that gently swayed outside my bedroom window was a play-mate by day but often a frightening figure of a bad man by night. This was exaggerated as it housed the nest of an owl and baby owls were loud and weird. I was afraid of the sound and slept with my head well hidden beneath the bedclothes. Twitt-twoo resounded ever after in my head.

The steading that was set aside from the house was always busy. I got used to watching cattle from the herd of champion Aberdeen Angus bulls parade in the yard. Dad was proud of his growing reputation as a breeder of these cattle.

By the time I was five years old I was taken to the February Bull Sales held in Perth market every year. One year there was cause for great celebration. The champion Estate bull was declared THE Champion overall. A beautiful beast he was too.

It was through taking an interest in the care of beasts that I began to look after my own little Shetland pony. This was a cute, sharp, bouncy, black six year old Sheltie and I loved her.

I was a confident rider who loved to ride in and about the steading. The men working there made sure I was safe enough until one day I fell off and Dad was alarmed. He told me I could only ride under the supervision of John Rugg who had moved with Dad from Chapelbank. I compensated for this ban by creating a stable of my own. I selected a range of long sticks as my 'horses'. These had to be fed and exercised every day. This occupied the little would-be stable girl as I groomed each one and gave each animal (stick) a special name.

Mum was alternately concerned and amused by her daughter's antics. "Do you think she's all right?" she asked Dad. He only laughed. "She'll make a fine horse-woman one day," he said.

Together Joe and Lily settled into their new life. In the beginning the move proved to be more successful than either of them could have imagined.

Then there was a surprise.

Joe looked at his wife with admiration and appreciation. She was blooming, he thought. "Daddy's special expression" I called it.

I knew by this time that there was to be a fourth member added to our family. Mum was pregnant with the baby due in the late

September of 1930, when I would be four and a bit.

Mum had an uncomfortable time. She was under the care of the local GP who visited but never examined her. Mum put on weight; her girth became increasingly difficult to manage. The baby was an extra large twelve and a quarter pounds. Like a beautiful three month old babe, his size took its toll on his diminutive mother. As a result Mum was sent to a nursing home in Edinburgh for recuperation.

The family was split up for a month or two. Dad stayed at home to run the estate and farm. I went to Bathgate to stay at Dunard with Auntie Nan and Granny, and the baby Andrew, Drew for short, was cared for at home by a trained nursery nurse. He was a contented bouncing baby and thrived on the rules of the nurse's philosophy which were very often very strict. The nurse would not allow me to run in and out of the nursery to play with my brother as I was keen to do and being sent away to Bathgate meant it took me a while to get to know him.

It must have been a difficult time for all the adults involved but the children were well protected. For me it was a happy time although I did miss my Mum, Dad and new baby.

This time away from the family at Bathgate set the foundation for regular extended holidays with Mum's sister, Auntie Nan. The Walkers at Bathgate formed a large part of the pattern of my future life. My uncles, aunts and cousins had a huge influence on my upbringing.

There were the grandparents, James and Lilias Walker. They raised a family of seven children, four sons and three daughters. Sadly

Nan's twin died before Lily, my mum, the youngest in the family was born, Grannie herself had had a twin sister too who died from the then prolific disease of diphtheria. Lily by her own admission was spoilt by everyone. As her daughter, I was granted this as a legacy by the extended family.

As one of my uncles told his own daughter, "You'll be alright in Bathgate if your name is 'Smith'; like mother like daughter."

The Walker business grew, eventually being likened to the first supermarkets in Scotland. It was created by the contributions from each member of the family and James Alexander Walker, Lily's father, had started the business.

He began working on the family farm in Lanarkshire and moved to become an Apprentice to his uncle who owned a butchery business in Princes Street, Edinburgh. When his Uncle retired James had sufficient savings and he bought a small butchery shop in Bathgate which was used to support the wider family farming businesses by selling their meat.

Finding jobs for each of his own children meant that the business inevitably had to grow and they did this, achieving a total of twenty two branches in the Lothians by the early 1940s!

To the butchery business the family added new departments: a Greengrocery, Grocery, Ironmongers; a Confectionery and general animal fodder sections.

These new business developments began when first James the eldest son and then the three younger brothers returned to Bathgate at the end of World War I. Nan joined the business at this point too becoming their Accountant. Only Lily did not join the business.

During the war Andrew and Johnny were sent to the Middle East as dispatch riders and came through the war unscathed. Tommy was not so lucky. As a medical student at Edinburgh University he was posted to a medical unit at the Western Front in Belgium. There he suffered a gas attack, the results of which affected him for the rest of his life.

James, as the eldest son, became head of the business and because the nature of the business was deemed to be helping to feed the nation he was excused from war duties.

Each of these men married and lived in Bathgate. So I enjoyed the company of my cousins:

James had two children, Inglis and Margaret, both older than me.

Johnny had two boys, Jaffrey and ten years later, Iain.

Tommy had Ronnie and Heather who were the same age as me and Drew.

Nan remained unmarried and looked after her parents until they died in the family home at Dunard in the 1930s.

This was the large family into which I was catapulted at four years old. It was during this time that I began to get to know my mother's brother, Uncle Andrew.

Uncle Andrew, the most generous of men, worked as a host in the Walker business. This suited him perfectly. He was affable and charming but he also liked to escape to play golf and so wove this into the wooing of new customers. Andrew was married to Jean Broome, also of Bathgate, and a baby was born to the couple just before I was born to Lily and Joe. Sadly, she was still-born. Whereupon Andrew became like a second father forever to Drew and me was beloved by us both.

I was happy to stay with Auntie Nan but my main companion was Jaffrey (Johnny's eldest son). He was three and a half years older than me and I thought he was the perfect champion. Through our childhood the games we played progressed from escapades in the back shop to playing golf and tennis or going for picnic walks together. It all began at that first visit.

Time passed, Mum recovered and the family back came together. Lizzie, the nursery maid, looked after both Drew and me and a happy atmosphere surrounded us all.

Occasionally though, little blips occurred such as the day Dad caught up with Lizzie, Drew and me when we were out for our afternoon walk. He stopped the car beside the pram with Drew in it while I tried to climb into the car beside him. I wanted to have a ride in the car back to the house. Dad told me to get out. I was to finish my walk with Lizzie, he said.

In return I was rude and cross and for once he reacted with annoyance, whipped me into the car and drove home in silence.

"Into the bathroom!" he ordered as he followed me up the stairs.

I waited apprehensively in the bathroom. Dad took his time and allowed his annoyance to fizzle out. Once inside the bathroom he plucked his leather razor sharpener from its hook and pretended to feel its weight.

"Hold out your hand!" he told me. Reluctantly I obeyed and closed my eyes. After a moment of stillness I felt the leather brush against my skin. It was quick and a gentle experience.

Three times he did it; each time was softer than the time before. The expectation of punishment was far worse than the one executed. Nonetheless that was the first and last time that Dad ever punished me. I was careful to obey him after that.

Chapter 4

Trips to Bathgate soon reduced to a holiday activity as I started in the Kindergarten at Morrison's Academy, an important first step into my academic career. I was six years old and my start at school had been delayed by a year because my parents thought me too young to make the trip alone. Going to school was an exciting adventure. First I had to catch the train at Estate station at the end of the farm road. The station in Crieff was on the outskirts of the town, just over a mile from the school. So it was quite a journey for little legs to manage. One day, on the return journey I decided to get off the train a stop early at Comrie. I went to the local taxi man and ordered a taxi home to the farm. Mum was so appalled that from that day forth I travelled to school by bus! My kindergarten years were cut short and spoilt by illness. I had what would be known later in the century as a viral infection. It first manifested itself as a sore throat, called a 'quinsey' throat. Then it moved to my ears, known then as a 'mastoid'. Finally, it centred on the glands in my neck making them swollen and tender.

The local doctor attended to me daily and his treatment was to recommend a poultice of a mixture of cement (anti phlogiston) to be heated then wound round the neck and secured there for half-an-hour. The applied mixture had a distinctive smell and seemed to be effective as the swollen glands became less painful. Nevertheless, the doctor continued to be concerned; he called for a second opinion.

He invited a specialist from Dundee to come to the farm and give his opinion. In the meantime, I was condemned to stay in bed.

Two things occupied me. Food was the first – I hated it! However, I resolved that problem by depositing my uneaten platefuls of good food behind the chest of drawers underneath the window. That secret hiding place was satisfactory in two ways. It immediately got rid of the food and it earned me praise from my mother for being such a good girl in emptying my plate, thus speeding my recovery.

It was only much later that the truth found me out. The smells of rotting food led Mum to the hiding place behind the chest of drawers. Secretly Dad admired his daughter's enterprise. He laughed.

The second thing was sowing marigold seeds out of the bedroom window and watching them grow.

I did not see much of my father. He was completely immersed in the affairs of the estate, the Home Farm in particular. That was where his special expertise was put to best use.

He was well versed in the modern developments of agriculture. He had exactly the right attributes for the job that McAndrew, the owner, required. In turn, Joe was lucky to have been recommended to McAndrew.

The two men respected each other and as a result the estate was known to be a model farm with the money lavishly available wisely spent.

McAndrew was a townsman from Glasgow, an only son of a highly successful shipbuilder on the river Clyde.

The demands of the Great War 1914-18 had stirred the beginnings of major growth of industry in Glasgow. Its port was in good working order and the hinterland provided easy access to the commercial and export trades.

Money-makers were on the lookout for new investments. There was one easy answer! Buy buildings and/or land. To do those things, one, or better still both, was to become an established member of the nouveaux-riche. McAndrew senior was a great admirer of his only son. He constantly showered him with presents but he had an extra special present to celebrate his son's fiftieth birthday. On that day he handed over a sealed envelope. "Good luck, son," he said as he handed over the 'deeds' to all his business interests.

The older man climbed back into his black Rolls-Royce. He gave a wave of his hand as he leant back into the luxuriously customised upholstered black seat.

"Let's go!" he ordered his chauffeur. "To Creiff Hydro." He lived in a suite at the Hydro until his death.

Mr McAndrew was constantly introducing new improvements on the estate. He negotiated with the owners of the Crieff to Loch-Earn Head Railway Company to build a small station, Dalchonzie, sited conveniently at the bottom of the driveway leading up to the farm steading. This was to facilitate the transport of beasts to the markets in Perth and Falkirk. It was also used extensively by the estate workers for shopping expeditions. Mr McAndrew and Joe worked well together, especially when Joe supported the idea of producing champion animals. He was keen to have good returns for his investments especially with Aberdeen Angus champions. With Joe the two created a well respected export market. New markets were created to the Argentine and South Africa.

Mr McAndrew acknowledged his lack of experience in agricultural matters. However, his business acumen was necessary if Joe was to succeed in establishing the McAndrew reputation.

The McAndrews lived in 'The Big House' built to their own specifications. It was beautiful Victorian-style, and was in keeping with a number of similar large houses scattered around that part of Perth-Shire. Such houses were mainly situated at the centre of their estate and surrounded by spectacular views. Mrs McAndrew modelled her ideas of a suitable lifestyle on the Duke and Duchess of York. Whatever the two York Princesses got, her children Pamela and Winifred had it too.

When the Principality of Wales presented the two Princesses with a miniature house Mrs McAndrew ordered the same model to be made for her two daughters.

When I arrived in the Home Farm there were hopes that I might find a companion in the McAndrews. However, Mrs McAndrew was quite clear that that would not happen. In her eyes there was far too wide a class gap between us. She acted like a superior lady having surrounded herself with the trappings of the aristocracy.

However, there was the occasion of Pamela's ninth birthday. It was to be celebrated by a small party to which I was invited. My afternoon began when I was picked up by the McAndrew's chauffeur driven

Rolls-Royce. I was six and was very much on my best behaviour. Mum had spelt out how important it was for me to make a good impression on the McAndrews. I was told I had to wait for Pamela and Winifred to set up how we would all play together.

The chauffeur pulled up at the front door of The Big House where one or two other young guests were getting out of their luxurious cars. I stood nervously in the entrance hall, uncertain of where to go or what to do.

Suddenly a young man in a grey uniform appeared. "Take off your coat!" he said quietly to me. "Then come with me to the nursery." He walked away with a bundle of coats draped over one arm. I followed him out of the hall into a room furnished with large, cushioned soft lounge chairs and sofas.

He walked quickly towards a door across the room. I felt that the other children were following my lead. I looked up as the man called out, "Children, come forward and meet Mistress McAndrew."

It was only then that I noticed a lady reclining on a pale gold coloured chaise longue. The most noticeable feature of the room was the magnificent ceiling. It had cherubs in each of the four corners with white handfuls of luscious grapes and cherries. There were two dozen candle holders hanging from the centre of the ceiling. Each point of light reflected on the long, carefully carved mirrors supporting a cluster of pigeons high on the walls. It was overwhelming. Young as I was, I never forgot it!

The party with Pamela and Winifred at the centre was ordinary but it ended in disaster. By now there were twelve children present in the magnificent dining room. A game or two (very genteel and quiet) had been played under the direction of the McAndrew Nanny. Full of suppressed energy, I jumped off my chair to collect my coat. My elbow caught a full jug of milk and sent it flying. The milk shot across the table to hit Pamela full in the middle of her designer, hugely expensive, party dress.

The girl leapt to her feet clutching her middle. Mrs McAndrew summoned a servant to clean up the mess. "You clumsy child," said Mrs McAndrew. I started to cry. My main fear was to wonder what my mother would have to say for such bad behaviour.

I wondered what awful punishment Mrs McAndrew was set on giving me. I tried to hide my tears and went bravely up to Mrs McAndrew to apologise.

I was astonished, though, when my mother having been told the story only gave me a hug.

"It was only an accident. It could have happened to anyone. And you remembered to say you were sorry. That was well done." I breathed a sigh of relief. "Grown ups are funny," I concluded.

Returning to school was both a pleasure and a trial. The carefree independent days vanished. A new routine was established. School attendance every day was required with no talking, no running about, no exercising my horses; in fact all the things I had spent the last year doing had to be squeezed into Saturdays and Sundays and holidays. My trapped feelings were only released by learning to read. Books were a revelation to me. Books and games! I loved them both. And for them I went willingly by train to Miss Oates' Kindergarten

Class at Morrison's Academy.

There, I sat at a small polished table with four chairs, cut to size. The only time I moved from my chair was at lunchtime. This consisted of a third of a pint of milk provided by the Government for health reasons and a slab of cheese with a thick slice of cold ham. I was not always hungry due to my recent illnesses but I always ate it all because Miss Oates would not allow any waste.

To sweeten the outcome I planned the use of my 'emergency' money that Mum always made sure was in my blazer pocket. I spent it on toffee which was taken back to Benheath, the girls' boarding house, heated and devoured by me and my friends. When asked by Mum what had happened to the money I would say that I had needed to spend it on a new pencil! She must've known it wasn't true because my face would give me away!

Morrison's Academy was the only fee-paying girls' school in that part of Scotland. It had a very good reputation for both academic achievement and as a boarding school. Many parents working in India sent their girls to Benheath Boarding House. The boys, a larger unit, had a choice of four boarding houses. They were all dotted through the town of Crieff. At the time the boys' and girls' schools were kept absolutely separate – except in the Kindergarten. There were some nice little boys who befriended some of the girls. Indeed one of own close friends married her kindergarten sweetheart.

I made a group of friends who have kept in touch up to the present day. There was Margery, and Rhona who were boarders at the girls' boarding house. Marygold who stayed in Crieff and I were day pupils and therefore the only ones with access to forbidden goods.

Smoking was the popular thing to do and the girls wanted to try it out. So, I was commissioned to get some cigarettes. This was an exciting commission. I soon managed to locate the cupboard where Dad kept his stockpile of cigarette packets. It was easy to detach a new packet when Dad had left the cupboard door open. I slipped it into school without detection. Triumphantly, I reported my success to the other three conspirators. The question now arose… where could the smoking safely take place. There was only one suitable place. I led the way.

"Just going to the toilet, Miss Oates," I told the teacher. I was unaware of the guilt written all over my face as I marched out of the classroom followed by my three partners in crime.

There were no others in the toilets so the four of us crammed into one space. Marygold produced a box of matches. Margery opened up the cigarette box and handed one cigarette to each of us. With much coughing and spluttering we all pulled on the first breath. Suddenly, we all froze. We heard the outside door into the toilet creak open. Someone was coming in. We looked agonisingly at each other, then followed Margery's example and pulled the hand holding the cigarette behind our backs. Smoke curled upwards above our heads. The toilet door swung open to reveal Miss Oates straddling the doorway, arms held akimbo. The expression on her face was grim. It broke my nerve. Again, the only person whose opinion mattered was my mother and what would happen if she heard about the part I had played in this escapade.

"Miss Oates," I pleaded, "please don't tell my mother about this, I'll never do anything like it again. I promise. I promise."

"I will see you all in my room in five minutes." Miss Oates turned to back off through the open door to the passage beyond. She gave a severe lecture to the guilty four but never referred to the matter again. As far as Mum was concerned, the incident was never reported to her and I was never in trouble because of it. After that Miss Oates was a heroine!

I was completely happy in the two halves of my life at home with activities planned by Mum and at school meeting up with all my friends. I loved wakening up every morning with the day about to begin stretching unknown before me.

I especially enjoyed reading and my favourite book of the moment was 'Black Beauty' by Anna Sewell. It was so good that I began to copy it out to make it more of my own. I could not count how many times I had read it. It was great to learn that it was possible to give horses a voice to tell their own life stories. I was intrigued.

Then there was school and all the excitement of things to be achieved with my friends.

Marygold had a box full of tartan coloured pencils. They looked beautiful and were so easy to use. I wished I had some too. Perhaps Uncle Andrew would give me some money to buy them. For now I would just have to make-do with my old cheap pencils and learn to write better. Anyway, I would soon be going to Bathgate for a holiday. There, I would be doing things with my cousin Jaffrey. What could be better than that?

Chapter 5

*I*n Bathgate Auntie Nan established the routine. On her way to work she took me to cousin Jaffrey's house. There I also had the spoonful of malt to ward off illness before Jaffrey and I escaped to do as we pleased till lunchtime. We went to see Uncle Andrew to 'help' with the shop's back room activities. A favourite task was to try to type letters or to collect the money from the shuttles arriving upstairs from the counters below. The noise and bustle was entertainment enough. Sometimes we went to roller-skate on a flat roof above the shop or stayed at home to play with Ian, Jaffrey's younger brother.

Auntie Nan took me home for lunch past the local primary school where all that could be heard was the chanting of times tables.

The afternoons belonged to Auntie Nan. There were lots of special visits including to the Zoo, to the 1938 Empire Exhibition at Bellahouston Park, Glasgow and trips to Dunbar and North Berwick to visit the cousins on holiday there. The time passed all too quickly and soon it was time to say goodbye.

It was always great and I was always sad to be back on the farm on my own. Then I had a good idea. I would go for a walk. I told my mother. I collected my school bag and filled it with biscuits, a thermos of juice and a wee brown bag from Nettie.

"Be back in time for lunch," my mother called as I departed through the back door.

It was a beautiful day; warm sunshine and blue skies. I hitched up my school bag. Imagining myself to be a real climber I set off up the gravelled track leading to a grassy slope at the back of the house.

This became my favourite walk. It went up the increasingly steep hill across a fast flowing burn. I had to remove my sandals and wade across as the erstwhile wooden bridge had been swept away. Once safely on the other side it was only a short way to the peak of the hill. There were full 180 degrees of surrounding views. For me at that age and stage views were mostly taken for granted, but these views were exceptional. I wanted to sit down to make friends with the birds that swept so effortlessly around the vast space – the occasional eagle, a few buzzards, even crows uttering their raucous squawking. And in between, the quiet silence.

I sat down by the burn and unpacked my picnic. Nettie always included a surprise – different each time! What would it be this time? I rifled about and produced a small brown paper bag. Carefully, I prised it open. A couple of walnuts and an apple fell out. A feast! I lay back into a soft bed of brown bracken.

Heaven had descended to the earth. I closed my eyes. This was my heaven and I relished it. Sadly time caught up with me. My mother had firmly told me to return by lunchtime. There was no use courting trouble. Reluctantly I stuffed my things into my bag and sprang to my feet. I ran all the way down the hill. I half jumped, half splashed through the burn's water and arrived, breathless in the kitchen.

"Hello," my mother said. "Had a nice walk?" There was no thought of child safety issues in those days. I was left free to do my own thing as I found fit. I used my common sense and enjoyed my imagination in the games I played by myself. I had no clue that this was going to be the day that changed the rest of my life. The drama took place in the lounge. It was a fitting place for such a dramatic event.

The scene was set.

Mum was sitting comfortably on one of the chairs, her current tapestry in her hands. She peered at it now and again to choose a new thread.

I was sitting equally comfortably at a table in a corner by the bay window. I was drinking a cup of milk and studying 'Black Beauty'.

Baby Drew was toddling about and examining things that caught his eye. Lizzie knelt near him to rescue him if he strayed into naughtiness.

All was peace and quiet.

Suddenly, there was the clatter of boots hurrying over the tiled hall outside. Quickly Mum stood up, her tapestry falling to the ground. Dad burst into the room. His face was scarlet and he was breathing heavily. He made for the fire then turned back to face his wife and daughter. "Whatever is the matter, darling? What has happened?" Mum went to him. She put her arms round him. "Come and sit down," she suggested and guided him across the room to sit by her.

"We are going to leave the estate. We cannot stay any longer. It is all about Mrs McAndrew and those chickens."

Joe disentangled himself from his wife's grasp and sat down heavily on the nearest chair.

Mum's face whitened.

As for me, not only had I changed colour but the milk turned sour in my mouth and I was almost physically sick. Leave the farm! To go somewhere else? Where on earth could we go? There was nowhere in the world like the farm. Surely, they would not take me to somewhere like Perth or even Bathgate? This was my home and that's where I was going to stay. I rose from the table and stomped away into the hall crying loudly.

It all happened so fast! Lily was anxious to move out of the farm house. She could not wait to say 'Good-bye' to the bully that Mrs McAndrew had become. For all its beauty and all Joe's pleasure in the farm and his success in breeding champion beasts she could not stand the way Mrs McAndrew treated her employees. Who was she anyway? And this final business over the size of the chickens was the final straw!

Mum went over what had happened and was glad they were leaving. Six plump, home grown chickens had been delivered to the Big House kitchen. Mrs McAndrew happened to be in the kitchen at the time. She demanded a certain weight of chicken and she weighed this batch as they were put on the scales. All but one was the correct weight. She was furious. She sent for the Hen-wife and shouted abuse at her. Dad was in the steading so heard there was a row going on. He made his way to the Big House and presented himself in the lounge where

Mrs McAndrew was holding court. That only made Mrs McAndrew worse. She told him he was responsible for the deficiencies of his staff. In this case his only option was to resign and therefore leave the estate. She told him that he and his family must go – at once. Dad felt he had no option but to leave and Mum did not need a second telling. She had never been spoken to like that and she was not going to allow it to happen to Dad either – especially not by a woman who thought that money could purchase anything.

In the nursery waves of the general unrest hit Drew and I. I was old enough to continue to feel upset and to wonder what was going to happen next. The only constant was attendance at school. But suddenly that changed too. Shortly after this the whole family moved out of the farm house. Dad drove us to Perth. Grandpa Smith had offered to house us until Dad found another job. Grandpa had built the first house on Kinnoull Hill, a big, typical Victorian style house which was Grandpa Smith's pride and joy. Everything had to be kept 'just so'. It demonstrated the peak of his hard work, his success and his position in Perth society. For him to have invited Joe and his young family to live there was unexpected but much appreciated. Mount Tabor had all the most recent innovations. It even had a telephone in the house which fascinated me.

Dad called his father 'The Old Man'. His mother, who had died a few years before, was a gentle person. Joe was the youngest of five children. Bob was the eldest, unmarried, and lived in London as head of a department in Liberty's. Frank was an accountant in his father's business but at a young age contracted TB and died. He was the father of Patricia and Erica. Rennie took on the family grain merchant business and had two children, Sandy and Betty. Mattie, the only girl in the family, married, and had a son called Gordon

Strang.

It was an unsettled, rather unhappy time. I continued to attend Morrison's. Some of this time was spent as a weekly boarder. I stayed in the girls' boarding house Benheath, under the direction of Miss Malcolm, who was in charge of PE at Morrison's. There were about twenty five to thirty girls with ages stretching between five and eighteen years old. I liked the arrangement and it was only possible because it was funded in the main by Grannie Walker. At the same time Mum had to adjust to a very different situation.

When she married Joe she had anticipated her own home and farm and living the high life, in Perth forever. Their wedding in 'Darlings Hotel' Edinburgh eight years before had been exciting and offered her a different new life.

The move into Benheath gave me a range of experiences I would not otherwise have had. It allowed me to consolidate the friendships with Margery, Marygold and Rhona and they are still friends to this very day.

On the domestic front things were not so good. Farms needing tenants in the early 1930s were difficult to find and money to buy a farm was certainly not available during the 'depression'.

Until Dad could find new permanent employment he was given a job by his elder brother and father in the well established family grain merchant business.

Uncle Rennie and Dad got on well together. Rennie was a good cricketer himself and was keen to see his younger brother doing well.

So, despite the worry of having no real job and a family to support Joe was able to enjoy an acceptable way of life.

Now aged eight years, I focused my energies outside of school activities, talking to Grandpa Smith's housekeeper, Jeannie.

Jeannie had a dog, a cute little grey-white cairn called Tattie who was allowed to rule the house. In particular Jeannie used him to get Grandpa to co-operate when he was being unmanageable.

Grandpa Smith was an irascible, obstinate 80 year old. He protected his actual years with a fierce verbal defence. I was afraid of him. He had raised his stick to me when I was just three and a half. I had bumped into a coffee table and lost my balance. He appeared very angry. Jeannie had to bring in Tattie to give the old man a barking and telling off.

I loved Tattie, who loved me back. It was the saving grace of having to live with Grandpa, especially as I knew how much my mother hated it. I wished and wished Dad could get a proper job.

A small move did become necessary and this did help to relieve the situation for my mother. Although Dad still had no new job the family were asked to leave Mount Tabor and find a house in the town. Instead we rented a house in Auchterarder. It was there that I acquired my identifying mark.

It was a Victorian house with a well laid out garden to match. Stone walls marked the boundaries where their garden was separated from the neighbouring land. There, great thorny rose bushes flourished.

Always ready to climb anything, I decided to walk along the top of the wall and see the garden next house.

It had been a rainy summer. Moss grew prolifically to cover the top surface. It was very slippery. Dauntless, I pulled myself up from the ground with small brother Drew watching with interest. I began my precarious journey. I picked my way. Then, without warning, one foot skidded. My balance was upset. I sat down on the wall with both legs straddling it, scraping down the rough finishing of the stones. As my legs divided, and I sat, astride the wall, my inner legs were scraped raw from top to bottom.

More seriously, my left leg had slipped between the wall and the thick stems of a central growth of roses. A pointed spear of branch pierced into the side muscles of my leg like a dagger.

I let out a squawk. Drew stared, his face intrigued. He was in a better position to see the damage. There was a gaping hole. No blood. Nothing broken, only a red hole. I took a quick look then hobbled back into the house with Drew at my heels.

Dad had just returned from a journey to England. He was talking with Mum about the possibility of a job there. As soon as he saw the wound on my leg he said, "Right! Cottage Hospital! Now!"

"I'll come too"! Mum's face had gone as pale as her son's. She was not good with injuries.

I intervened. "I want Dad to take me. It will be interesting!" So far there had been no pain. Only the hole. I was amazed at the lack of blood. Maybe I was dying!

"Come on." Dad swept me up in his arms to go in the car.

In the absence of the appointed doctor who usually manned the Cottage Hospital, the Matron decided to insert the stitches to hold the gaping gash. She was not well practised. She fed in a needle and tugged through a thread. Now I felt it. "Oow!" I wished the doctor would come quickly. He must be better than this ham fisted woman.

A total of forty eight stitches were sewn in to try to pull the skin together. It was a difficult job as there were no clear cut edges. It was more like a tear. The scar was there for life.

However yet more change was closer at hand than the family realised.

One day at the end of summer as the family sat at tea Dad came into the room waving a letter.

"It's come! At last!" he announced. "Got it! A job! The one with Suttons Seeds based in Reading. How about that!"

Mum ran to give him a congratulatory hug and kiss before he picked me up to give me a hug too.

It was true! To Reading we were going. This was completely unknown territory for each one of us. This was the 1930s and a job was a job worth having in any part of the country. That was the deciding factor in agreeing to leave behind family, friends, all that was familiar and take a step into the unknown.

Chapter 6

R eading! From Perthshire, Scotland. From one end of the spectrum to the other. How different could things be! At least Mum and Dad knew the ropes and those they did not know they soon found out. For the first time they were on their own with both families, particularly the Walkers, forced into long distance support. This they managed well and my connection with Bathgate remained as strong as ever.

The train came into its own although at just eight years old I was still too young to travel alone. I was otherwise well occupied trying to adapt to going to a new school.

Mum was familiar with the English education system. A trained PE teacher, she qualified from Anstey College, Birmingham and subsequently taught at Skipton Girls' School for four years. She finished teaching there to join the staff of George Watson's School for Girls in Edinburgh before marrying. But things had changed as she recognised, and in haste a school, Malvern House, was chosen for me.

Drew attended the Junior section of Reading High School for Boys. He had begun his education in Auchterarder Primary School. So this new, large big school was full of very talented pupils. It had a glowing reputation and provided many introductions to a wide range of games and sports in general. His potential talent was nurtured and developed. The cricketer in him took root. His interest and enthusiasm being thus fed and watered, he grew and flourished.

However not all confidence building activities were as successful as had been intended. One Christmas Mr Short, the Headmaster, introduced a new item to capture some boys who were musically endowed but who did not play an instrument. Drew had a good singing voice. That first Christmas the Junior School put on a concert. He was allocated a singing spot. He had to sing a duet with the Headmaster. The piece was 'Good King Wenceslas'. Drew sang with a tenor level while his partner had a bass tone. They did not blend well. To add to the humour that boys in the audience found irresistible was the discrepancy in their heights. Drew, even though he was tall for his age, was only about three feet whereas the Head was exceptionally tall, at about six foot three. They looked a comical pair. The episode did nothing to boost Drew's confidence.

I, however, was enjoying an easy life at Malvern House. I was put into a class where I had already passed that standard of work. The classes were small, the teachers indulgent and I sailed along. My ability in sports singled me out. I enjoyed being a winner but Mum was not so happy. She and Dad thought there should be more challenge. In every department they wanted me to be stretched not spoon fed.

By the end of the first year in Reading Mum had researched other schools and had come to the conclusion that a different school was a 'must' for her daughter. The 'Abbey School' had all the right credentials. So I was enrolled there.

It was known as an excellent school for both academic and sporting achievement and success. Its emphasis on high standards, values and general education made the school more than comparable to the best girls' schools in the whole of the country.

In addition Mum and Dad found and rented a house where the garden marched alongside the boundaries of the boy's High School playing fields and The Abbey School playing fields lay just beyond them. I could walk to and from home to school without treading on a pavement.

The school was a two storey red brick building. The teaching was of the highest order. There was an outdoor swimming pool with water polo included on the curriculum. I was welcomed into the final year of the Middle School. The girls in it were clever, pleasant and willing to be friendly. Friendships that were made then continue to the present day and Sheila still never forgets my birthday.

There were various events which appealed to me. One of these was a reading competition. This was open to all Middle School pupils. I entered enthusiastically. On the day I returned home at lunchtime to collect my bicycle.

Head down, legs pumping hard I set off round the road to school. I did not want to be late nor did I spot that a van parked in my path had opened its back doors. I failed to judge the space available for me to pass. I caught the pointed edge of the open door. Blood poured from a deep cut above my left eye-brow as I fell off my bike to land in the gutter. The van driver was oblivious to the accident and drove away. I tried to mop up the blood. I retrieved my bike and turned towards home. My only thought was that I might miss the reading competition. But I did not miss it. Mum saw to that after Lizzie had patched me up.

By the time my name was called I was collected enough to read well and I won. The only problem left to solve was my bicycle. It had been bashed and the string that I had carefully tied to the handle bars had got tangled.

I had arranged thick string round the handle bars to represent the reins of a horse. It was a similar idea to the way I had harnessed up in my 'stables' in the farm garden. It worked brilliantly on the bike. I sat well back on the saddle, and guided the bike by using the false reins. I had the control of the machine down to a tee! However after this escapade I was confined to using shank's pony for a while!

Both Lily and Joe had come from churchgoing backgrounds and Joe went to the Congregational Church and Lily to the Church of Scotland. There was no discussion about attendance. That was taken for granted. Sunday was for attending Church in the morning and going for a walk in the afternoon. Therefore, the habit continued unchallenged after they were married.

In 1934/5 in Reading the Congregational Church was the most vibrant. So, the Smith family became members with Dad soon becoming an elder. Drew and I went to Sunday school. I also attended a 'Crusaders' group on a Sunday afternoon. Therefore, it was expected for all of us to take part in any current activities.

One Sunday, the Minister – Rev. Vine – announced a competition organised by a Trust.

The Trust had money to sponsor the gift of a specially tooled Bible to the pupil who could recite a chosen collection of extracts from The Old and New Testaments in the shortest possible time. The Minister was to be the judge of who was the winner. I was immediately interested to enter.

At lunch that day the whole project was discussed by the family. It was thought to be a good idea. Then, Mum added an additional motivation.

"Tell you what," she said to me. "If you can win this Bible you can go to Bathgate. How about that?" There was only one answer. "Oh great!" I tackled the task right away. But where could I get privacy to learn the verses? I had one absolutely guaranteed private place.

... THE TREE!

I rushed out into the garden and stood beside the trunk of the ancient oak tree. It had always intrigued me. It was so old, so thick, with leaves covering its spreading firm branches and so easy for me to climb. It would make a comfortable hiding place. Sitting there I could see all the people and the action that was taking place in my own garden as well as the goings on in the neighbours'. Ideal!

I liked sitting high up in the tree and learning the verses did not prove to be too difficult. I learnt the listed passages within the next two weeks. When I went to the Minister to have them judged he told me I had a good memory and that I had come first and therefore I became the winner of a beautiful black leather bible.

More than that I had won a visit to Bathgate and the holidays would begin in two weeks.

The Abbey School was geared to pass exams in preparation for entrance to universities all over the country. However, it also paid attention to other aspects of educating growing teenagers. It suited me, and I suited them.

The PE staff trained at Bedford College of PE, were lovers of hockey. They were led by Miss Thursfield. She was heavily involved in the English ladies' hockey scene and she was a current English national team selector,

She must have approached meeting a fresh, ignorant group of middle-school girls with the prospect of enthusing at least some of them with her own wish to play.

If that was her aim, she certainly succeeded! I loved playing hockey from the first touch of the ball. My hand-eye co-ordination had always been good. Dad had honed that skill from an early age. The pair of us had stood out in the garden for hours throwing and catching a ball. At the same time usually with a cricket ball – Dad would be practising his wicket keeping. It was good preparation for both of us and drew us closer together.

At school my class was a group of, go-ahead girls. These traits came to fruition later in their lives when eighty percent of the careers they followed were based on offering help to others. They were enterprising, responsible and confident leaders.

Hockey became a major influence for me. I was lucky. Every opportunity that fell into my lap just seemed to arrive there without much effort on my part. There did not seem to be any agonising decisions to be made.

It was a happy little group of girls running round in the May sunshine during the second year of World War II. Few of us knew much about it. Of course we knew it was not a normal easy time for adults or for some children and two evacuees from London did, stay with us for a short time before their mother arrived to take them back home. Although Reading was west of London it was in the Thames Estuary and received its fair share of nightly bombs. It was an odd choice of town to house evacuees.

Every night the whole of our family trudged down to the bottom of the garden and settled themselves in the four bunk Anderson Shelter. Overhead, on the dot of 8pm, everything on the surrounding grounds stopped. The lights went out and silence fell as all the incarcerated population fell quiet. Then, from the flights of German aeroplanes flying above came the distinctive beat, beat, beat of their engines. The clear sound of the enemy was unmistakeable.

I held my breath, shut my eyes and listened to the radio which was always turned on. Even I was able to recognise the ultra English tones of Lord Haw-Haw as he poured out a stream of propaganda. I copied my parents' example and laughed. It all added to the evening's entertainment.

The bombing of London every night began to take its toll not only in destruction and death but in the minds and physical energy of the population. The bombing seemed never ending yet education and the attendance of children at school continued in the usual way.

I had only one near direct encounter with real danger.

One day in May 1943 I was walking home from school. I had reached the middle of the High School's rugby pitch. I was in the centre of a large area of open grassland, very vulnerable and totally unaware of any danger.

It was a dry, sunny day and I was enjoying the heat of the sun as I skipped along towards home lying just over the dividing wall.

Then, suddenly, first in the distance then quickly moving closer was the clear sound of aeroplane engines. I stopped sharply and listened. There was a German plane approaching fast. Behind it came a Spitfire. Then I remembered the BBC News. The Battle of Britain (as it was dubbed later) was taking place in front of me; the fiercest of the almost hand-to-hand battles was right there – above me. The two planes were swooping and climbing in the space right above my head.

One pilot claimed the room that had been created. The other got as close to the rear machine gunner's position as possible. A burst of bullets stopped any further manoeuvring and both planes wheeled away from each other to the safety of the open sky.

I stood still as both planes seemed to sweep directly towards me. I found myself looking straight into the German pilot's eyes. For one second only. He unlocked his gaze when a spray of bullets aimed by the rear gunner of the Spitfire pumped his gun.

I felt a moment of panic. Where to go? What to do? To run or stay put? To cry or to shout out loud?

Events overtook me. The German limped out of sight and ended with a big bang that indicated it being written off.

Several teachers witnessed the dog-fight and my predicament and they rushed from the school to the playing field to take me into safety. For a short time I lived off the story – until more exciting episodes took the school headlines.

In school the next day I was encouraged to tell the class my 'story to tell'. This was the period in school when a pupil recounted a new or recent experience.

Chapter 7

Parts of Reading were badly hit by the nightly, mostly stray bombs. There were air-raid shelters and I practised evacuating from the school into them on a regular programme. Otherwise there was little interruption to the smooth well organised running of the school.

Hockey matches were the excitement. Other schools were played and beaten. I advanced by leaps and bounds. I was selected for the first school eleven when I was just 13. A natural centre forward I was prominent in scoring goals. On one occasion I scored eleven goals in a win of 12-0!

My ability was noticed by the old girl's club, 'The Scarlet Runners'. It was a strong, successful club and at age 14 I was playing regularly for their first team. It was a great thrill to be thus promoted. It was particularly special because the person in the centre-half position was Miss Moir who had been selected to play for the English Midlands! Wow! You can't do much better than that at 14!!! It was a wonderful introduction to the highest level of play and paved the way for further rapid improvement in the years to come.

It is amazing how one thing creates a platform for the next thing. How it just happens – it makes an offer and all you have to do is say 'Yes' out loud. At least this is true of my life!

This period of life attending the Middle School of The Abbey School was remarkably tension free within the constrictions of a country at war. There were hidden tensions at home but I was not fully aware of them. Dad and Mum never allowed their personal concerns to spill over in a way that would affect their children. However, it did not mean there were none.

Dad had been plunged into a job in which he had little experience. He was buying and selling grain, drawing on his recent time in the family business. At the start he knew no-one. He did not even know the geographical position of the farms he had to visit. Mum accompanied him in the car to act as navigator. Between them they managed to build up a clientele. Berkshire was an attractive part of the country with the River Thames running through it. I found my home life was dominated by Lizzie. Mum had advertised for a kitchen maid when she went to live on the estate. Lizzie, from Falkirk, was fourteen at the time. Jeannie taught her the ways of the kitchen and how to manage the cooking and baking. Lizzie had been at the farm for all the years with the Smiths and had become the main childminder. Her major interest was Drew; she had been in charge of the baby after the nurse left. From then onwards she looked after him. He loved her and she loved him.

Lizzie was part of the family. Where the Smith family went Lizzie came too. She had never been further away from her home in Falkirk until she arrived at the farm. It was a big upheaval for such a young girl. But she coped with the total changes in work and status and now in Reading she was almost able to be entitled 'cook-general'.

Mum had never contemplated Lizzie leaving our family, especially as she was more essential than ever for the running of the house. It came as a great shock to Mum when she sent Lizzie home to Scotland for a holiday but never returned to Reading, explaining this in a note saying she had been too homesick.

It was just another hurdle to overcome.

All the time the war rumbled on.

At the same time, the war was becoming more personalised. Reading was no longer just a dumping ground for bombs not unloaded over London. The reality of 'London's Burning' was only too true with the smell of burning filling the atmosphere.

Then the 'doodle bugs' appeared. They were frightening. There was no knowing when and where they might land.

We struggled to maintain a calm normality. School was able to achieve a more even keel than we were managing at home.

Dad and Mum constantly discussed the possibility of sending Drew and I by ship to the USA or Canada. It was a risky business but once the Atlantic was safely crossed boatloads of people would be safe for the remainder of the war.

I did not want to do that. Drew was too young to fully understand the implications of what would happen. Dad and Mum swayed this way and that. Then, their minds were made up for them. News came through that a ship, crammed with children, had been sunk by a submarine.

"That's it!" Joe folded up the newspaper with the awful headlines on the front page.

We stay together! We live or die together! No more talk. Let's get on with things here, good or bad. I could forget the possibility of being evacuated. Thank God.

Relief flooded through me and better still I was going to Bathgate for the holidays.

Auntie Nan was equally glad to hear of the decision. To celebrate she had me to stay and the war receded. However this was a less successful visit than usual as Jaffrey did not have as much free time as in the past. – he was about to leave school and had a place at Edinburgh University. Jaffrey was called up but was first allowed to follow his degree course at Edinburgh University. He graduated with an MA and then he rejoined his regiment as a 2nd lieutenant.

In Reading the Smiths followed their own paths without too much drama. Little seemed to change but the wider impact of war was immense. People we knew were killed and wounded but for me the importance of school and the fascination of new subjects as I learnt more about them blotted out everything else. Exams began to loom a bit larger on the horizon. English and History emerged as my best loved subjects. Maths and the sciences had much less of an appeal – probably because I was not as good at them! Latin was hard because in my year at Malvern School I learnt no Latin and this put me well behind my contemporaries at The Abbey. Yet I knew that a condition of entry to university depended on a pass in Latin. So, head down! Concentration at a peak. It could be done.

Another, unexpected, source of activity came to the fore and it came in the form of babysitting.

There was an elderly lady who attended the same church as the one chosen by us. She was always on the look-out for newcomers or visitors and tried to make them feel welcome. At the beginning she smiled and chatted to Mum. As we were all regular attenders on a Sunday gradually we all got to know each other better.

It appeared that the old lady had continued to live in her family house with her daughter. This was not far from our house. It was a well built Victorian building standing in its own grounds.

One Sunday her daughter invited Mum and I to join her tennis party and have tea in the intervals in the tennis. I was flattered; I was a good tennis player and had played with the best players at school but I had not played with adults. This would be very different. I comforted myself that they must consider me to be good enough to be able to play with them. Nervously I joined them. To my surprise I enjoyed myself. According to the feedback on my performance, as reported to Mum, I had acquitted myself very well. I was delighted to accept a second invitation for the following week. As usual Dad summed it up best, "It was nice to get to know such a good family and also be able to play a game to a decent level." Dad was keen to foster any potential in games that his children might have inherited.

Yet there was more to come through introducing me to the Butler family. Old Mrs Butler had a new grandson, just christened Richard. Baby Richard made an indelible impression on this not quite teenage girl.

I had had little to do with babies. I felt I had missed out on helping in the nursery with Drew and that I didn't get the chance to bond with him early on.

Richard Butler had the most endearing smile. And he was just lovely. I fell in love with him from that very first tennis afternoon.

His mother Muriel was delighted to have the help that I was only too pleased to offer. I bathed Richard; dressed him; supervised his sleeping; pushed him to the park – in fact, I spent as much time as possible with him. He was such a good baby. He never cried but had a gurgly, infectious little chuckle. Mum was amazed and if the truth be known, a little nervous about the responsible things Muriel allowed me to do!

Then came the day of change; several things that could have sunk my happy boat. They didn't. However, a little shudder did give my confidence a small knock. The first was that Dad chose breakfast-time to make his announcement. He said, "We're moving back to Scotland." The words fell into a pool of silence, cold and unwelcome. Mum and Dad were tired of being in a shelter every night with bombs falling unpredictably round about.. No thanks when we had been offered a nice house in Crieff to move to.

"What about school? Especially for me. And the exams?" I exclaimed.

Dad had all the answers. He and Mum had obviously thought about a move to a safer area of Britain. Not only would it be safer to move back to Perthshire, it was home country for Dad. He knew many people; he was comfortable in the land. He had already found a job and a house to go with it. Morrison's Academy was virtually on our door step again. Everyone in the family was catered for. It was the sensible thing to do. Dad was absolutely sure. I was less happy.

What about school, I had immediately asked? Not only did I worry about the academic side of it, there was the hockey. What chance would there be for playing in a good team? I was now just fifteen years old. I had my new friends and now I would have to start all over again in spite of knowing some of the girls I had originally known in the Kindergarten. Both they and I would have moved on.

All this was made more difficult after Mum told me that there would be a delay in the whole family moving into Milnab House. I could not afford to lose any time at school and so I was to be boarded out with a local doctor's family for the first term.

Before that happened Mum came up to Crieff to supervise the arrangements. This included going to be interviewed by Miss Mason, Head of Morrison Academy Girls' School.

The lady was of the traditional style; her manner was formal and formidable. She questioned me about my level of education and never referred to my beginnings at Morrison's Kindergarten. Then she lapsed into a lengthy silence.

At last she began to tell us her decision. She told me that she was going to put me into Senior 3. That was a year below the pupils I had originally started school with. It meant I would know no-one. I had been demoted, put down before the term began. Tears welled up in my eyes. I felt humiliated. Mum asked the obvious question. She could see how upset I was.

"Miss Mason," she began. "Why are you putting Marie into such a low year? She has been doing well in the equivalent of senior three already at The Abbey. And the Abbey has one of the best academic reputations."

"English education, we find here, is exactly a year behind the Scottish standards. Therefore Marie must automatically go into S3."

Later there was no alternative for me but to accept the situation. In practice it meant that according to my age for leaving school with others of the same age (eighteen) I had no opportunity of having a 6th year. I left school after sitting my set of Higher subjects in 5th year; It all levelled out though after the next period of higher education at the beginning of a career qualification.

The familiarity of the buildings and the friendship of Margery, Marygold and Rona all helped me get over the loss of all the good things left behind at The Abbey and in Reading. I missed Richard and his new sister. There were no other 'Butlers' in Crieff to replace them.

In my class I made another good friend. Elizabeth Sime. She was a boarder at Benheath. She came from Broughty Ferry. She was a great friend to me and made my life at Morrison's enjoyable. We shared an interest to do well academically although Elizabeth's bent was languages rather than mine which was in English and History.

I proved my ability in English when the class was entered into a national essay competition in 1943. 'Fires Helps Hitler' was the title. I won the regional section and won a prize of some National Savings Vouchers.

As a celebration Elizabeth invited me to stay in Broughty Ferry during the Easter holidays. There I was introduced to Gilbert & Sullivan and 'The Mikado'. It was the dominating music of the holiday and gave me a first taste and a love of the theatre.

In my final year at school I took part in two school productions. 'Beauty is in the Eye of the Beholder' – a 'straight' play in which I played the lead role. The second production was a musical based on the ballet 'The Nut Cracker'. I loved the music and the part I played – the old toy maker.

These diversions in my last year at school were balanced by playing tennis for the school. Marygold and I made a strong partnership and won all our matches. That achievement was recognised at the school prize giving on the last day of the summer term. The Head Master of the Boys' School told the audience he had an extra prize to be presented. He produced two top class tennis racquets and announced that the winners were the unbeaten two girls.

It was a nice accolade for us both as we moved on into higher education.

There were hockey matches but with war restrictions biting harder than ever, transport was a great problem because of the rationing of petrol and in many cases no petrol at all. But problems are there to be solved – so it is said! In this case it was surprising how many farmers suddenly took an active interest in their daughters/cousins/ sisters who had to be helped to get some exercise such as playing hockey! Amazing to find the enterprise and creativity that emerged round the parishes of Crieff and Auchterarder!

It was an incentive to have had a Glasgow school, Laurelbank School, evacuated lock stock and barrel from Glasgow to Auchterarder House for the length of the war.

A half-way venue was agreed. The laden cars set off to meet at Muthill. The excitement was great especially as the hockey match promised to be a close result. Laurelbank was known to be a good hockey school.

Teams of children were squeezed into the available cars and many matches were played that day. The time chosen for this day was early in the autumn term. The weather was generally kind but it would not have mattered had it been soaking wet. It was a tremendous day out for both schools and Morrison's ended up winning.

The day with Laurelbank School was not only for sport. The breaks between matches and the opportunity to meet 'the other side' were seen as equally important. The girls made full use of this time and many friendships were forged.

I was fortunate to meet Jean Sloan. We immediately found we had a lot in common, not least a common interest in playing hockey. Jean played to school level but little did I know then what an important person in my life she was to become.

Chapter 8

*T*he choice that faced me during my last year at school was between reading history at the University of Edinburgh or Physical Training at Bedford College of Education. It was a difficult choice as I was drawn to each with equal enthusiasm.

The fact that Mum had gone to Birmingham to Anstey College and qualified in Physical Education may have been an influence. Her assessment of the various colleges in England and their reputation had been established over the previous forty years. Anstey specialised in dance; Dartford in games; Chelsea – more general; Bedford – in games; and Dunfermline offered the only generalist course in Scotland. After studying all the literature it was clear that Bedford would be the best one for me. But that College was one of the most popular – would they offer me a place? With a recognised annual intake of between thirty five to forty students, places were scarce. I waited anxiously for a reply to my application. It came at last, but it was conditional upon a selection interview.

The letter was from Miss McMinn, the College Secretary. It was an invitation for me and Mum to meet this lady in the lounge of the Balmoral Hotel, Edinburgh on a given date.

I was nervous especially when Miss McMinn asked me to give a demonstration of how I walked the length of the hotel entrance hall.

This was to show my posture and general bearing! I must have met the criteria as I was immediately offered a place in the coming first year of college.

The College was made up of a series of old houses, some detached, some terraced, which lined one side of 37 Landsdown Road. A big rectangular building occupied some of the opposite side of the road. They were used for dance and gymnastic classes. At the rear of all the residential houses gardens stretched out to access the road running parallel to Landsdown Road. The gardens had been converted into netball and tennis courts; there were also two newly built classrooms.

The playing fields were marked out for hockey, lacrosse, cricket and athletics. These open spaces were sited about two miles away on the edge of Bedford's town boundary. They were easily reached as every student owned, and constantly used, a bicycle. That, apart from the legs, was the form of transport.

Bikes were in demand when it came to reaching teaching practice assignments too. Even the staff relied on their bikes.

The students' common room boasted a large slate notice board. One day an elderly member of staff left a message on it which said: "Would someone put away Miss –'s Bike!" Some time later the bike was still in the wrong place and later still, the bike was away but there was a new message: "Miss – can put away her own bike!"

I, of course, had no idea of the geography of the colleges. The biggest and original College building was No. 37 Landsdown Road. This was Miss Stansfield's residence as well as being the administrative centre for Miss McMinn and the College dining room.

I knew that it would be a long journey on the day I travelled from Edinburgh to Bedford. But I had not measured exactly how long. At least I had new white gloves on my hands when I set out, black when I arrived from the filth of the steam powered train,

I boarded the train in Edinburgh – LNER – and reached Bletchley twelve hours later. I still had to catch another local train to reach Bedford. At 9.30pm I stepped out of the train and onto Bedford Station.

There, standing in silent splendour, stood a girl very like myself. That surely must be the senior student who had been nominated to 'befriend' this strange Scottish lass who had taken nearly fourteen hours for her journey. It was a very long way from the home I would not see again until Christmas!

The welcome I got from my new acquaintance was warm enough and I was shown into what turned out to be my 'home' for the next few years.

No 29 Landsdown Road was a three storey house with an attic on top. My room was a single, narrow little attic room. It was rectangular furnished with a bed on one side and on the other by a small Victorian open coal fire. The door opened out onto a small wooden internal stair leading down to the main staircase. A notice was pinned to the side of the wall housing the fire. It read: "This fire can only be lit on a Saturday after 6pm. Similarly, on a Sunday. A ration of coal can be collected on a Saturday morning from the cellar." The coal rationing of the nation-at-war was bitingly effective.

Everywhere was cold, icy cold, but some venues were worse than others. The swimming pool was a good example.

The winter of 1947 was particularly severe with ice covering exposed surfaces to a depth of feet rather than inches. Year III students were timetabled to have swimming. They assembled at the pool slipping and skidding with every step. There was no heating either inside or out. The group were confident there would be no lesson on that day. They underestimated the member of staff's dedication to duty!

"Get changed, girls!" was the command!

Followed by: "Jump!" And everyone did! The cold was indescribable!

I vowed I would never voluntarily swim again!

However, this was all ahead of me as I landed in 29 Landsdown Road on a pitch black night in early October escorted by a weary third year student. I was given a plateful of salad and told to assemble in the dining room at 8am the following morning. The door gently clicked shut and I was alone in a strange world where silence and lack of human activity ruled.

Tears threatened but what was the point?

I thought of the interview in the Balmoral Hotel – how Mum had laughed with me. I wished Mum was with me now to share this laugh – a lot more grim. Still, there was only one thing to do. Deal with it!

I felt shattered, so 'bed' was the solution. I fell onto the hard, narrow bed. For a cover I used the thick, heavy blanket-like double-lined cape that Auntie Nan had made for me. How thoughtful she had been. How Auntie Nan spoilt me. We had a great relationship and I just loved Mum's sister to bits. With that thought ringing round my head the next thing I knew was a gentle pair of hands shaking me.

"You'd better get up. You've to be down for breakfast by 8am. You'd better hurry. I'm Joyce, by the way."

And that set the tone for the next three years.

It was non-stop, physically exhausting, mentally demanding, emotionally challenging and academically stretching.

I was drained of all my resources by the end of every term. This was recognised by Mum and she dealt with it in a way that allowed me to recover. She gave me breakfast in bed having allowed me to have a 'long lie' to sleep it off. The month-long holidays at Christmas, Easter and even more weeks in the summer provided the rest that was needed.

I was not well prepared to meet the curriculum in the first year. There were thirty five girls (you might call them 'young ladies'). This was a good-sized group. They all had at least one talent that matched an activity in which she could claim to be better at or at least equal to all the rest. It was a competitive world.

I looked around that first morning as the group went through the various activities. To me, the others were all so good, so confident, so experienced. The war did not appear to have spoilt or damaged their willingness to try out something new.

My main weaknesses spanned gymnastics and dance. All my

contemporaries had gone to English schools, in the main, fee paying independent schools, their PE curriculum included coverage of the basics of gym and dance whereas I was more versed in Scottish country dancing.

The PE person at Morrison's Academy was only interested in that. She was also a very good player of Scottish Country dance music. Her playing reverberated throughout the school. The girls loved it and left school well taught and knowledgeable about the national dances of Scotland. But that was of little use to me where most of my fellow students had concentrated on 'modern' dance and gymnastics. The traditional dance included English Country dancing about which I knew nothing. It was a nerve-wracking situation. I dealt with my ignorance by 'shadowing' one of my friends who was an expert in movement. I hoped I would be hidden from the steely eyes of Miss Reid who missed nothing. Nothing was ever said to me about my poor participation – that was not the way that problems were dealt with at Bedford College! The view was that students were quite capable of solving their own problems. And that, 'my dear student', was character building. Therefore, I was left to my own devices to do the best I could to catch up.

As a result I practised with two of my friends. I would never be a wonderful dancer or an acrobatic gymnast but I became sufficiently competent to be an accurate demonstrator able to teach dance and gymnastics.

The other subjects that took up half the timetable were games – hockey, lacrosse, netball, cricket, tennis and an introduction to the 'new' fashion, basketball and handball. Swimming and the ability to swim, was a condition of entrance for every student.

Those were the personal performance aspects of the daily 'fitness' regime. I had no difficulty with any of them and excelled at several. Hockey was my main talent and I was soon playing for both the College First XI, and the English Midlands XI as their centre-forward.

I quickly represented the College as a first team member of the tennis and cricket teams too. At that time teams had matches against adult clubs and other PE colleges. All these fixtures made for a busy and strenuous life. Yet, I was delighted with it and would not have changed it in any way.

Of course, the very serious training – as a teacher in PE – operated parallel to these activities. There was intense academic input in the form of the sciences, anatomy and physiology. First and second year medical coverage had exams approved by the University of London. I even enjoyed the smell of formalin throughout the dissecting department.

These subjects were over and above the courses on child development, modern studies, the history of PE, the role of the teacher and up-to-date papers from Denmark and Sweden that were leading contenders of PE in Europe.

More was to follow for me and my year. The qualification in massage and exercise was inbuilt into the main PE course. This meant that a student leaving Bedford was also a fully qualified physiotherapist. Aiming at achieving this dual qualification gave the students energy to sustain the extremely hard work.

I found the staff encouraging and dedicated. Miss Stansfield had set a standard of integrity and values that were lasting and as the students were more or less hand-picked and as the staff were nearly all Bedford-trained these principles were upheld.

None of these views were ever spelt out in words, they were just absorbed. I started on this journey by myself that night. That first term in No 29 Landsdown Road was a tough – or, toughening – experience. Miss Goodridge was the resident member of staff. She was strict and unbending. She was head of the dance department and better with third year students than first year. Her room was a ground floor room so all residents had to pass her door to reach their own.

The bathrooms were shared. There were no cooking facilities or sitting room provision. I sat in my own little room, alone with my cloak draped round me – especially when it was icy cold and I was sitting up on the bed.

The whole house was bitterly cold. The students were timetabled for every minute of the day so it was only during the supper time between 5.30 on to bedtime that the occupants found the rooms unbearably cold in winter. Extra thick jerseys and woollen jackets together with hot water bottles and mittens were the order of the day. It was essential to spend that time meeting the demands of the course including memorising 'Gray's Anatomy'.

There were nine students in the house who all became good friends.

I had Joyce, Chris, Fay and Bridget as my particular friends. They were a group of firm friends throughout the College years but more than that, our friendship has lasted through the years. They have all taught, married, had children and kept in touch with each other. I found them very supportive and interested in my family and activities.

Members of staff were a breed of their own. There was a distinct hierarchy of seniority from Miss Stansfield, Founder of the College and still its Principal during my first year.

Miss Stansfield's successor was Miss C M Reid. There followed a line of experts in their field, very experienced, Bedford-trained lecturers. Finally there was the youngest member of staff, Miss Hilda Hammond.

Hilda Hammond left College to teach for three years at St Malvern boarding school. She was invited to join the Bedford staff at the end of that time, head-hunted by the Principal. Hilda's specialism was hockey. Although unknown at this time, Hilda and I each played hockey against each other for England and Scotland respectively.

With such a full timetable there was little time or energy left for students to enjoy a social life of their own. My group made our own entertainment under that heading. I cast, directed and produced 'Peter Pan' and 'Oliver'. The rehearsals had to be held at 6.30am – the only free time for the cast. It was fun and the final result was worth the effort of getting up at such an unearthly hour.

This use of time available was adopted by Miss Reid when she organised and produced the whole year in a women's health and beauty demonstration in partnership with Bedford Community. Fortunately these early summer mornings were dry and warm. The tarmac on the 'parade' area was not too cutting on bare feet.

The idea supported by Miss Reid was aimed at working with Bedford Community to benefit all.

The College recognised the demands made upon the students and that was compensated by the introduction of long holidays. I was fully occupied during these days. Together with Mum we walked into Crieff through the McCrosty Park. This was a pleasant walk, and good for Darkie, a black cocker spaniel who accompanied Mum wherever she went, the most exotic place being the football match on a Saturday in winter. There he curled up behind Mum's legs and kept her warm! Dogs were always an integral part of the household.

In the holidays I played tennis for the Crieff tennis club, often in the doubles with my brother Drew. He and I also played in the Scottish Hard Court Championships at St Andrews. We reached the third and fourth rounds over several years until we stopped in 1949.

St Andrews was an attractive place for holidays. There was plenty for teenagers to do and Drew and I did them all.

Outside College, I was the lucky one. Just as in Reading I had a local 'family' of my own, The Foys. Frank and Muriel Foy were a young married couple who had just bought a house in the road behind the college. They had just had their first baby, Caroline, and they opened their doors to me and any of my friends who cared to visit.

I took full advantage of this kind and generous offer and used the Foys' house and home as my own.

The way that Muriel and I knew of each other went back to Crieff and a series of coincidences. Muriel Foy's mother went to Crieff for a short holiday and stayed with a friend of my mother. In conversation it emerged that my mother mentioned that I was beginning my three years as a student at Bedford College. This story was relayed to Muriel who contacted the college about me. Thus began a life-long friendship between me and Muriel's family.

Frank, Muriel's husband, had a neat brand of dry wit and scepticism regarding physical exercise and sport in general. He kept my feet on the ground. We all got together on a Sunday afternoon especially in summer. We all had bicycles and cycled leisurely along the flat paths of the Canal. Jennifer, their second daughter, was added to the collection. Her seat was in the front basket of her father's bicycle. She loved it and laughed and gurgled all the way to the special picnic spot where we could spend the afternoon. Ideal!

Chapter 9

The days passed quickly. They were tightly held within a cycle of work discipline. The greatest excitement was to sneak out to indulge in a cup of coffee at the corner café but that did not happen very often – too expensive. Again I was so lucky. I was given a ten shilling note each month by Aunty Nan. I used it mainly to post letters home and for other everyday necessities. Often when writing home Mum and I compared the differences in our courses. There were a great number of similarities with Mum's 1915 – 1918 course: the same full timetable; the same curfew; the same treatment; the same lack of meeting with the opposite sex.

In Mum's social calendar her boyfriend rode a motor bike, driven by the Minister's son from Bathgate. They met round the corner of the College when he was on leave during WWI.

My boyfriends of WWII were confined to paper. I received over 100 letters from India in my three years at Bedford from my Scottish boyfriend, who was posted to there. When he was sent home he came straight to Bedford to propose to me but I found I could not accept his offer. There was great family disappointment all round as he was a favourite at home but it was not to be.

But I get ahead of myself. College life continued apace with hockey fixtures taking precedence.

My place in the College 1st team gave me the opportunity to play in trials for the English Midlands team.

Hockey was a very popular game all over the home nations. It was also a major game across the whole of Europe.

The Midlands team played against the other English regions. National selectors attended these games and selected players to go forward to specific national team trials. Hilda Hammond (Moore), member of staff, and I were the only two Midland players to go forward to the next level. Of course, being of Scottish nationality, I was not eligible to go further. But nor did it mean I was automatically transferred into the Scottish potential international group.

In Scotland the clubs across the land played each other in leagues. Players were selected to play for their regional team, East, West, North, South and an additional team, Anglo-Scots. This team accommodated those like me with Scottish nationality who were living and playing in England. A big tournament was held on the 27th, 28th and 29th January each year. The games were played in St Andrews and occasionally in Troon. The international selectors sat through every match and made their choice of players for two teams, the 'Possibles' v the 'Probables' with two extra players to be reserves. The wait before the team was announced was fraught! A reserve eleven was also pencilled in to play in an annual reserves tournament played at Old Trafford.

When weather permitted I practised my skills in the garden in Crieff but no designated coach existed. A manager saw to all the travel arrangements but had nothing to do with the players regarding tactics training and the games.

The chair of the five selectors was the most powerful position. The selectors were quite a sight as they huddled at the side of the pitches. They were wrapped up in mohair travelling rugs with woollen hats pulled over their eyebrows, trying to look knowledgeable as well as stay warm!

After my first tournament I was selected for the 'Possible' side. I was 18 and as a student I had to go to see Miss Reid, the College Principal to get her permission to play. It was an intimidating experience!

"Enter!" Miss Reid instructed.

I entered.

"Yes?" Miss Reid did not lift her head.

"Well?" I tried again and I explained my offer.

There was silence. Prolonged silence.

At last Miss Reid lifted her head and looked at me.

"Come on, girl, I haven't all day. Is that it?"

I nodded. All the pride I had felt vanished. I was deflated.

"Well, Miss Jaffrey Smith, I hope you don't get selected. That's all I can say. You are far too young!'."

That wish expressed by Miss Reid was accepted by the selectors and I was named on the Reserves for that first trial. However, I was subsequently re-called for the next international against Ireland, played in Edinburgh.

In those days there were only three international games a year and these were all home country games against England, Wales and Ireland so opportunities to play for your country were very fairly limited.

The fact that Bedford and Crieff were so far apart geographically made it impossible for me to go back home during the term except for international matches! Most students expected to be in the college boarding houses for the full term, only going home for the holidays.

I was immersed in my own world as I progressed through my second year but the war did intrude from time to time. I knew several boys, R.A.F. mostly, who had fought the enemy and had been killed in the Battle of Britain. I also knew young men at school who joined up immediately on leaving school and who had become seriously injured.

Distance from the family was especially difficult to bear when there was bad news from the War.

In my third year I was grateful to have just arrived home for the Easter before Mum had to break to me the news that Jaffrey had been killed in Belgium.

I wanted to know the details but no-one knew any. There was only the stark fact. No more. I was numb. I could not believe it. My darling Jaffrey.

A corner of this foreign field that is forever Scotland. For no good reason a misquotation of the famous poem rattled through my head.

The days that followed were bleak. I remembered all the things I had done with my cousin. We had continued to see each other even as the years passed and we both grew up.

Gradually, details of his death were sent to his parents. They were comforted by letters from his Major and later came the real story from his batman.

Evidently he had taken a jeep to cross the newly built bridge over the Rhine. The British army were doing well. A permanent crossing was to be established, therefore Lieutenant Walker had to find billets to house his men for the night. His batman offered to accompany him but Jaffrey refused. He knew the batman was exhausted and told him to put his head down while there was time. Then he set off. Not far along the road he met head-on a jeep full of drunken British officers. Jaffrey was killed. The Matron of the local field hospital also wrote a note. She said he had died peacefully. I only hoped that he did.

On returning to College I was kept very busy and this helped to dull the pain of the loss. The time flew past.

Miss Reid, the Principal, was keen to involve the students with some war work. To that end she signed up some students to go to a farm outside Bedford to pick peas.

I was included in a group of students to make a start on this physically demanding task. A lorry was sent to the College about 6.30am and the girls piled in to the back of it to be carried out to the field where the peas were ripening profusely.

It was good fun but it was not made clear that this gesture really prevented the nation from starving to death!

Other parts of the College curriculum were dependent on the co-operation of the Bedford students. There was mutual respect and a very good working relationship between Bedford Council and the College. Teaching practice was dependent on being allowed into schools in and around the town.

The cottage hospital also provided patients for the final year's Massage and Exercise certificate.

My participation in the final treatment of patients in Bedford was to treat a patient with a severe condition of paralysis. She was completely bed-ridden as her legs and arms were locked and unmoveable. She found the exercises and gentle movements that I introduced to be painful initially but they had further effect of loosening up the joints as the days passed by.

I enjoyed this medical side to my PE qualification. Some students changed direction altogether and moved to take a physiotherapist course. So there were strong links between Bedford Hospital and the College.

All these many strands to our work provided a steep learning curve for the students. Jam-packed! Even if there was a 10pm curfew it was no hardship because everyone was so tired by the end of the day that they made their own curfew. The exhaustion grew to such an extent that by the end of the term all I wanted to do was to sleep!

Some of the holiday weeks were taken up by a placement booked by the College physiotherapy department. This was to gain experience in dealing with groups of patients. I went to Gleneagles, the erstwhile world-wide railway hotel turned into a convalescent hospital for soldiers. The wounded were mainly amputees who had to learn to walk again. Therefore the atmosphere was positive and hopeful. I was driven there every morning and collected every night by Dad. I worked all day in the Physiotherapy department. The patients felt they would soon be discharged so they were full of jokes and banter. It was a happy place to be. I enjoyed it and was fully occupied for two summers. The end of the war was celebrated in 1945. There were various functions held all over the country.

I was at College the day peace was declared. There was a feeling of relief, of joy, of happiness. My group of friends caught the back of an open lorry into Cambridge. The streets were seething with people, people singing, people dancing, people shouting and people jumping.

It was a release from six years of war.

Public acknowledgement continued. In Crieff, it was decided to present an entertainment in the Public Park centred on the Victorian bandstand, with people representing different sections of society in Crieff. As a recent ex-pupil of Morrison's Academy I received an invitation to speak on behalf of the youth of Crieff during the war.

This was an honour; Mum was greatly pleased and together we made up a speech. It was a daunting task. One that I approached with growing apprehension. I had never used a microphone before; there would be a big crowd and my nerves jangled.

The day, when it arrived, was dry and bright and I managed to keep my nerves under control to get through it.

Despite my work with soldiers at Gleneagles I had mostly shared a sheltered life with a group of like minded girls and broadly speaking we all regarded men as a separate, often unknown but intriguing species. The ways of getting to know and understand them were many and wonderful.

For us as students from all girl schools we were expected to conduct ourselves properly and respectably and so were our young men. Girls and boys were segregated at school and the rules about getting together were strict. However we did find ways of getting together despite the rules, or perhaps because breaking the rules was fun!

In spite of our youthful anxieties about the opposite sex the vast majority of the students did marry and have a family.

My experience with boys started on my return to Morrisons aged 15 and I gained quite a lot of attention. That was quite exciting. First the note arrived via another girlfriend: 'Would you meet me to go up the Knock?' This was the gentle hill that rose up behind Crieff. Another note followed suggesting a time and place to walk safely beyond prying eyes. Then the long anticipated 'date' finally arrived.

I made my way to the 'popular' place! That first time I was nervous but not half as nervous as the boy. It showed and I was well aware of it and did my best to put him (Tom) at ease. As a result we were soon more relaxed and the jokes began. After about an hour we finished up on the promise that we would repeat the experiment. I put him at the top of my list so far! He was a nice enough lad! A rugby player, quite a good one too and by a strange quirk he also went on to become a dentist like my husband!

Tom was a couple of years older than me so as soon as he left school I was free again

No. 2 was a tall, very fair, charming 6th year boy. Neil Sturgeon had a great asset! He drove a neat little car. He stopped at the end of the road where I lived. He dispensed with the 'note' routine and went straight for the jugular!

He stopped the car beside me, pulled open the passenger door, and said, "Do get in. I'm sure you would like a lift to school? Right! Fine!"

"It's a small world. I think our parents have met. So, you must be OK," he added.

And that was the start of a good friendship. It led to taking part in other events such as the May morning walk. This Senior four took place early on 1st May. A group of boys went round certain houses early, 5am, on that day and threw gravel unto the bedroom windows of selected girls to waken them. The girls joined the boys waiting below. Then, together they walked down to the river Earn along Lady Mary's Walk where they paired off and then all came back together again to complete the walk.

The first time I was selected in this adventure ended in disaster. For the first, and only, time in my life I fainted! Probably a combination of excitement, empty stomach, and the need to impress the opposite sex.

I could feel it coming on as the group walked towards the river. It was a horrid, out of control sensation and then nothing! I woke to find one of the boys helping me to sit up and then get back onto my feet. He supported me back home. That was the end of my 1st of May walks!

At least my year did not indulge in climbing in and out of the windows of the boarding houses as a future generation of boys started to do visiting the girl's boarding house. If only the resident staff had known what was going on under their noses when they thought their charges were innocently fast asleep. Meetings at the school gates was adventurous enough for me!

No 3 was David Rennie who, having watched me play at Hockey Camp at Ballater, fell head over heels. He even cycled all the way from Dundee to Creiff to meet up!

At College students were treated similarly to 6th year pupils and directed accordingly. We were given no opportunities to meet boys and as a result No 4 was a relationship conducted at long distance by letter.

My final year at College flew by. So much to do, so many exams to take, theoretical, physical, and teaching. My friends and I turned our attention to job hunting in general terms. I was sure something would turn up. What did happen was amazing! As with my life to this point and thereafter I did not seem to have to take strong action to achieve something good. At the right time the right opportunity just seemed to happen for me.

Chapter 10

One day early into my third year I was summoned to Miss Reid's room. That message always made me feel nervous! However, on this occasion Miss Reid was pleasant and conciliatory. "Please sit down, Miss Jaffrey-Smith," she said. "By the way, you notice I continue to call you 'Jaffrey-Smith'. We have done that during your time here to distinguish you from all the other 'Smiths'!" And that became my adopted surname from that first day at college until I got married

"I would like you for the post currently free at St Leonard's in St Andrews in Scotland. I think you would be admirably suitable. It is a very prestigious job. I am sending you and Joan Reeson for interview. St Leonard's always takes Bedford trained PE people. I will endorse your application. Try to be a little more confident and report back to me when you get back to college."

"Thank you, Miss Reid." Miss Jaffrey-Smith was duly impressed by the attention given to her by the Principal. I composed a letter of application to St Leonard's and anxiously awaited a reply.

It arrived promptly one week later.

It was the middle of January 1948. The winter had descended on Scotland with a vengeance. Everything was frozen. Roads were covered with snow and then turned to skating rinks. I was still on Xmas holidays from College but I had to get from Crieff to St Andrews for 9.30am to be in time for my interview. I had been at a party the night before which had not finished until late.

The party had been held by the Sturgeon family and was an exciting whirlwind affair. It was unique and something I was not prepared to miss.

The Sturgeons were a family of three boys, very attractive, who lived in the beautiful Ochinflint House. It was only part of the house at that moment. The war was to blame for the change of use. A school owned by Mrs Sturgeon, originally based in Dundee, was evacuated to occupy Ochinflint. The school remained there for the whole of the war and functioned successfully for several years afterwards. The whole enterprise added to the attractions of Crieff especially as it was an all girls school which added possibilities for liaison with Morrison's boys.

Mum became good friends with Mrs Sturgeon. That became an important relationship several years later.

I knew the Sturgeon's eldest son Neil well. He was in 6th year to my 3rd but there seemed to be no big gap. He was a charming boy who went on to be a most successful doctor in Canada.

The party held at Ochinflint was in honour of his birthday. I got little sleep after I arrived back from the party so I was glad Dad was driving me to St Andrews that day.

It was a horrendous drive. The car was a grey Hillman – noisy, unstable and bumpy with the snow chains on the tyres to prevent skidding. Dad was a good driver and he had to be. Despite the winter tyres the number of skids were countless but at least we remained upright which was a miracle in itself. We reached St Andrews, intact. Then, to find the right part of the school. Only half-an-hour late. There, Miss Strathearn awaited us; she was an older lady. In her day she had been Head of PE at St Leonard's and Bedford-trained Then she had moved onwards and upwards to be the Secretary to St Leonard's. Like a bodyguard she stood between me and the Headmistress, Miss MacFarlane. She held the floor while the other candidate, my contemporary, Joan Reeson, arrived and were then joined by the current young PE teacher.

I turned my attention to the orders being given by Miss Strathearn. I caught the last sentence: "And we shall enjoy it all from seats in the balcony. Thank you, Miss Jaffrey-Smith." She began to walk towards the office door. "Miss Reeson you may sit with me until it is your turn to teach," she told the other girl pleasantly enough.

"Got it!" I quelled my rising nervousness.

It meant Joan and I were to teach alternating classes presumably all morning while the older group sat in judgement and decided who was best for the job.

The main difference between Joan and myself was that Joan was a lacrosse player. Speedily I scanned the group to try to decide who would lean towards the lacrosse game and those who favoured hockey. Of course there were other important factors such as teaching ability, personality, background and in the meantime the job in hand was to keep the pupils moving to stay warm and to do a good teaching job. I was given little time to prepare. The classes came to the gym without a pause. Each group for 10 minutes of exercise, bang, bang, bang. The gym was a surprise to me. I had expected it to be up-to-date, modern, with new apparatus. To be easy for teaching. Not a bit of it. It was tiny with a balcony occupying one end – quite low and seating about eight spectators. It had the air of being very old – nothing had been renewed for a long time. And if the car had been cold the gym was twice as bad. The thing to do with the pupils was to heat them up and leave them perspiring.

At the end of the first session of classes I felt I had done that; the children obviously enjoyed it all. I thought it had gone pretty well. I was sure I had not stuck to 'the Book' though but I had taught for the good of the children and they had benefited. In contrast I understood later that Joan Reeson had stuck to the book and her classes left the gym as cold and correct as they entered it.

I agreed to wait philosophically. But there was more to come. I had never played Hand Ball, very similar to 'Fives', but hitting a small ball with the palm of the gloved hand instead of a racquet against four walls was more like playing squash. Yet that afternoon at St Leonard's Joan and I were put onto a 'Fives' court to play a game against the present head of PE. She was an excellent games player from being Scotland's centre-half for many 'caps' to this rather, medieval game of 'Fives'.

Then there was a swift tour round the buildings and premises and they were impressive. St Leonard's was a boarding school for girls; they lived in a number of large Victorian style granite stone houses set amid beautiful grounds – including hockey and cricket pitches, tennis courts and gardens. The view over the sea at the east end of

St Andrews only enhanced the beauty of the setting.

That guided walk was a joy and sealed my hope that I would be given the job. But I was not optimistic. No hint was given before the two candidates left that evening. I returned to College where an anxious group of friends waited to be given a blow by blow account of our ordeal. Miss Reid was given a watered down version!

A week to the day an envelope lay in the hall. It was addressed to Miss Jaffrey-Smith. A similar envelope lay beside it, addressed to Miss Joan Reeson!

Lying there side by side they told – nothing! I studied them. I should lift the one addressed to me. Dare I open it? Footsteps sounded in the corridor. That was enough to give me the necessary motivation and I took a quick step towards the table to snatch up my envelope. Hastily, I made my escape to the sanctuary of my room. There, I ripped open the envelope and unfolded the paper. The typed letter came into focus. My hand steadied and I read the typed sheet. Immediately, my eyes were attracted to one word – '...offer...'

I read it all again and this time it made sense. I was being offered the job! Fantastic! I could scarcely believe it. On the staff of St Leonard's! I could not wait to tell my parents. They would be pleased. So would all the people in Bathgate, especially Aunty Nan. I had a passing sadness thinking that Grandpa and Grannie Walker would have been proud too but they had died in 1932 and 1935 respectively.

Chapter 11

*I*n the long holiday before starting at St Leonard's I discovered an idea that Dad had for me. It was meant to be a secret but somehow it leaked out. Drew adopted it as fair game for a good teasing issue. I was not over pleased at his kind attention!

The idea was quite simple. I was to marry, and to marry a farmer! I was not averse to the idea and I would've liked to live on a farm again. There was one big snag: my dad's interpretation of who would suit me. He had selected the farmer in question.

Alistair and I were introduced but for me no bells rang. Yet Alistair was a decent chap. He was a wealthy sheep farmer, pleasant companion, looked good in a kilt, well educated and kind. He was immersed in sheep and was a successful breeder who was much respected in the farming world. These were essential ingredients in the small but influential agricultural community round Crieff. All these characteristics were positive and Alistair could not have been a better candidate for Dad's big promotion as a prospective husband for me. Yet, my answer – privately at that stage – was, "Sorry Dad, no way, nice as Alistair is and he's very nice to me. He's not for me!" Alistair tried one last throw of the dice! – a real country dance. This was to be held on the steading at his farm, in the washed and painted barn with food served on the ground floor and mainly Scottish country dancing taking place on the first floor.

In a crisp, moonlit night, the dance began.

All Alistair's friends from near and far danced the night away replenished by food, washed down by barrels of beer. It was a great night. Alistair made his infatuation known but I stood firm. "No, dear Alistair – No!"

Dad was disappointed so I felt guilty. I was not quite sure why except there was a kind of heaviness in the air. And it was my fault. I was sorry but to have agreed would have been wrong. It was a good dance all the same!

There was a new life awaiting me at St Leonard's. I graduated from College and prepared to put into practice all I had learnt. On my first day I met up with Miss Andrews, my head of department. I was quickly introduced to her method of communication. It was unusual!

It was a message from her to me written on St Leonard's best writing paper . Thereby she gave directions regarding the day's teaching.

The pattern of the notes, which were beautifully written, was the same every day.

To: Miss Jaffrey-Smith

9am – 12.30pm: *Classes in the gymnasium*
                         – Teach gymnastics / Dance as you choose

2pm – 4pm: *Hockey*
                         St Nicolas Versus St Leonard's Fields

Fives

Tennis
Day Girls Versus East House

The Captains will

(i) Select teams
(ii) Ask for special coaching.

Any questions – ask the House Captains.

In case of rain: Country Dancing in Hall. (This is unlikely as girls are encouraged to be outside every day.)

Captains will meet you on the correct pitch.

Finish sharp at 4pm.

I had not anticipated this kind of partnership with my senior. However it soon became a very comfortable routine, especially the part played by the House Captains. I really was treated as a respected, all-knowledgeable experienced coach. I got to know the girls and they all enjoyed these afternoons of games.

The social side of life for me was not neglected.

St Andrews was very familiar to me because of the many years I had been there for a month at a time for the family summer holiday.

I wandered round the town to refresh my memory of those times.

I walked the length of Market Street up to Hope Church. There, I could recall the occasion when Dad seemed to be walking very slowly towards me. I must have been nine or ten at the time. He was arriving in St Andrews from the farm where he had been gored by his Friesian bull. The family were all in St Andrews but he was left on the farm. The bull had got loose and chased Dad to catch up with him and pin him against a wall. A small stable boy, the only other person at that moment, ran in front of the bull to distract it from doing further damage. Fortunately he succeeded. Dad suffered a few broken ribs but it could have been much worse. The bull was monitored more carefully after that! It certainly alerted Mum to the potential dangers for those who work on a farm.

St Leonard's provided a house to accommodate the resident staff. The staff house was in South Street just at the back of the school building. It was an old, substantial house beside the arches. There was room enough to provide eight members of staff with a room each, plus a very nice sitting room, two bathrooms, a kitchen and a sun-bathing flat roof which was totally private. There was a resident housekeeper, so no effort to housekeep or cook was required by the resident staff. We had complete freedom to do anything that caught our fancy and with my short teaching schedule even more so. I also had a built-in companion. The first person I met as I opened the front door of the South Street was Jean Sloan. There was mutual amazement and pleasure.

"What are you doing here?" The question came from both of us at the same time. The answers followed, "I'm on the staff!"

That was the beginning of a close and long friendship.

Jean had been appointed to the languages department. She had graduated from the University of Glasgow and this was her first job too.

Jean and I were the two youngest in the staff house. We enjoyed all the activities we shared especially the long walks along the sands, east and west and going to the Byre Theatre. This was a great pleasure as it really was truly an old byre with the smell of cattle continuing to linger in the front seat of the stalls.

In school the girls were delightful. I enjoyed teaching in the cramped gymnasium. It was a challenge that the girls shared making the lessons more fun. The afternoons were sheer joy. The different teams performed against a backdrop of the open sea and sky.

At the end of the day there was always a delicious supper, often with my favourite recipes, especially the chocolate éclairs.

The evenings were always full of interest too. The senior residents knitted, sewed, painted or made something that was useful and creative. I could knit and I began to be more enterprising in turning to Norwegian patterns. My gloves in particular were much admired.

During these evenings the radio played gently in the background. That was our staple entertainment. Otherwise there were outings, concerts, visits and a mixture of social events. The war was over and people were looking for something exciting to do.

Mine came first on a motor-bike!

Charles was a native of Cupar. He was a garage owner and 'into' anything on wheels. He was the cousin of one of my colleagues in the staff house and he asked me out. I was to share the seat of his smart, fast motor bicycle! It has to be said the members of the House held up their hands in horror. This was too dangerous with no protection, too fast and any objection they could think of piled up in front of me. I ignored them all. When Charles came to call his vibrant revving of the engine could be distinguished the length of South Street.

Well warned by Charles to wear something warm.

I swung a leg across the pillion seat – much to the mixed emotions of a group of St Leonard's girls, ranging from suppressed giggles to open-mouth admiration as they watched from their vantage point on the opposite side of the road.

Mum and Dad (modern parents!) were not sure which line to take, out and out disapproval or mild acceptance. They hoped that Charles would move on. Riding on a wave of enthusiasm Charles and I rode all over the countryside whenever we both had time off. Loch Earn was a favourite spot especially the west side along the bumpy road.

Charles would ride from Cupar to collect me and take me via Comrie to St Fillans. We would ride the few miles to Loch Earn by on a Sunday where years before Drew had nearly drowned.

He was about three years old, a non-swimmer in a blown up ring. He thought it would be great fun to swim to the island in the middle of the loch. Mum gave chase but that only made the bold boy go faster. It took her a good quarter-of-an-hour plus a man in a rowing boat to pull him to dry land.

Nothing like that happened to Charles and I.

Sadly, one day Charles announced that his father had bought a new garage company in Cornwall and had given him the job of managing it. It was an offer he could not refuse. There was much talk and a few tears. Charles was keen to turn friendship into marriage but fun though our relationship had been it would not, for me, last to the forever that I knew I would expect from marriage. So, we parted and I went back to knitting my 'Auntie-Nanigan' cardigan obviously for Auntie Nan!

St Leonard's was lovely if you fitted in and I certainly fitted in! I felt respected and welcomed there and sometimes even appreciated. The school was games minded and hockey was the game. Lacrosse was played but in a minor key. Hockey held pride of place. The head of PE, Miss Andrews, an internationalist herself, wore her Scottish Team purple blazer every afternoon to carry out her coaching. Therefore when I won mine I wore mine too.

Socially it was great. The housekeeper, Miss Pouts, produced imaginative meals and every person's favourite was catered for even although the eight lady members of staff were more interested in the subject they were teaching than in the food they were eating. Then there were the walks all round the sands of St Andrews. All this topped by the rides on the motorbike's pillion.

After Charles left my Air Force friend Donald whom I'd known since childhood came to stay for weekends and take me out for dinner. It was with him that I broke my previously strong alcohol code. It happened one Saturday afternoon when we went out for a run in the car.

"Let's go for a coffee," he suggested. "There's a nice hotel on the way to Elie." We made our way into the car park and walked into the hotel. I was sitting while Donald ordered. I examined the drink when it came. "Pimm's No. 5" I was told. "Very good for you! Here's to you! Maybe you'll change your mind after that!" I examined the fruit piled into the alcoholic liquid. "You mean about marriage?" I asked. "No, I don't think so – not even if you get me tipsy!" But I did enjoy the drink!

Chapter 12

Dad was very proud of his children. He encouraged us both in every way and took immense pleasure if we succeeded. He and Mum watched my hockey matches whenever possible and Dad's knowledge of the tactics and 'reading' games was a great asset. He was a primary mentor for me. Cricket was his all-time favourite sport. He listened to 'Test' match commentaries and took the family to Lord's, the Oval and Edgbaston as well as to the North Inch in Perth.

With such a companion to explain the nuances of the cricket it became a well understood philosophy. This was the case not only in the Smith household but across central Scotland.

When Dad played for the Perthshire County side they achieved 10,000 spectators every Saturday on the North Inch and for a local derby game against Forfarshire this number could easily more than double. Perthshire were a first-class side from 1925-1935 and even entertained Don Bradman, the Australian named the greatest batsman in the world at that time.

One Saturday towards the end of the summer term I invited Dad to St Leonard's to watch an inter-house game. He was delighted to accept. The standard of cricket was high because the girls played their cricket against university sides and Ladies Clubs because no local school played cricket. As Dad was in the vicinity he decided to call in to see a Perth Junior side in Cupar. There he met up with the Hutchison brothers, Frank and Bill. They farmed the family farm behind Cupar and they both played cricket too. Dad arranged a meeting between Bill and I. That was so successful that we began to go out together. The residents of South Street House observed with interest the development of this relationship.

However Bill's mother had other plans for her younger son and our meetings grew less frequent. The continuity of our relationship was not helped by my own timetable of hockey matches.

The very first international in which I played was in March 1948 on a school ground in Edinburgh. It had been snowing and was freezing and a white ball was easily lost in the snow so instead an orange ball was used. In that game I had an inauspicious start. The ball was passed to me on the Right Wing. I put down my stick to receive it. The ball approached at speed. Just before it reached the stick it hit a lump of ice, gave a little hop, did a jump in the air, cleared the stick elegantly and rolled defiantly over the sideline. I had given it to the opposition. The crowd groaned. I was mortified; my first international, my first pass, my first chance, and my first mistake!

Perhaps if the team had had a supervised warm-up I might have been better equipped to deal with my first touch (or miss!) of the ball.

Nevertheless I was gradually and increasingly being chosen to represent Scotland and was selected to play for Scotland in the Festival of Women's Hockey in Amsterdam in May 1948.

As the War came to an end this was one of the new and exciting explosion of activities to get sport quickly back onto inter country peace agendas.

It was 1947 when the IFWHA (International Women's Hockey Association) announced a World's Conference to take place in 1948 to be held in Holland, and Amsterdam would be the venue.

In view of the way that the city had fought to survive during the war was wonderful enough without taking into account the extra stresses and strains that it had to face internally now that peace had been restored. To provide the organisation of a World Conference would make it even more special for the countries that would take part.

Scotland gladly accepted the invitation to be part of this brave event.

I was selected to play. It was my first foray into the echelons of playing hockey abroad. Eight teams, one from Belgium, Ireland, Holland, England, Wales, USA, South Africa and Scotland gathered in Amsterdam and the tournament got underway. It was a round-robin style of competition where each team played everyone else.

Scotland and indeed most of the other teams comprised older women who had played hockey before the war and whose career had then been cut short.

It was a marvellous setting in Amsterdam in the hottest weather. The Scotland team played well. Although the youngest member of the team, I did not seem to be out of my depth and I scored a number of good goals, so much so that we found ourselves in one of the semi-final positions. Unfortunately we did not make the final but in the play off for the Bronze medal we played against Belgium. Amid cries of "Allez Belgique" from the crowd Scotland battled through and won by 2-1 so we were winners of the Bronze medal.

I have kept this medal carefully over the years and mine looks the same in hand today as it did on that blistering podium in Amsterdam. I think this is still the only time Scotland has been the winner of a medal in a World Championship.

*

That tournament was a good start to a post-war surge in the promotion of hockey in schools, colleges and universities.

This was a significant point in my life. I was no longer a child or a youth and launching into adulthood was a mix of being a daunting prospect and an exciting adventure. I had safely achieved qualifications. I had left exams, assessments marks and all the paraphernalia of student life behind and was ready to tackle the new sets of challenges brought by young people, new colleagues and the requirements of my job teaching in a prestigious boarding school.

The days flashed by and St Leonard's generously continued to provide time for International hockey fixtures. I represented Scotland in games against Ireland, Wales and visiting teams from Holland, USA and South Africa.

There was also time for a social life. I felt so lucky to have met up again with Jean Sloan. We became firm friends, sharing many interests and supporting each other through teaching and leisure activities. So when Jean suggested going to France during the long summer holiday of 1949 my immediate response was an enthusiastic 'yes! Marvellous!'.

We planned the holiday with Jean being the prime mover as she had spent a year living with a French family whilst doing her languages degree. As a result Jean was a fluent French speaker unlike me who at best would need to rely on schoolgirl basics.

There was only one small impediment to our preparations. Mum did not think that this was a suitable trip for two unsupervised young women travelling to a country recently ravaged by war. Mum was sure that the toilet facilities would be appalling and the accommodation generally poor. Besides how and what would we eat considering that rationing was still in force in Britain. Nevertheless we followed through with our plans.

We went first to Southampton by train and from there by boat to Cherbourg. The Channel crossing was a smooth one offering fantastic views of the coasts of both Britain and France. The fine weather did not last though. No sooner had we stepped ashore than the heavens opened. Neither of us had prepared for such continuous torrential rain. Our rather natty collection of summer clothes including fashionable long shorts did not protect us from many a soaking. The bus to our Guest House was a welcome relief from the rain.

We settled into the first part of our holiday but abiding long in my memory has been the nature of the food. Guests were seated at strongly smelling wooden tables and served with every meal were home grown tomatoes. These had leather-thick skins and were doused in oil. I was 'scunnered' and found it difficult to eat anything at all! It was with higher expectation that we started the second part of our holiday travelling to Paris.

As soon as the train left Brittany the weather changed. The sun shone. The rain vanished and the heat arrived. Paris was bathed in unbearable heat as the two of us made our way to the Youth Hostel which was to be our home for the next ten days.

The Youth Hostel was jam packed with foreign students (mainly male). It was noisy, smelly, and dirty, with iron bedsteads and thin mattresses. It was well outside our normal comfort zone.

Escaping to the many tourist sites of Paris and for as long as possible was the agenda for every day and we enjoyed all the sights.

It was not the beautiful French holiday for which we had hoped. It was an experience and certainly cemented a life-long friendship between us two girls.

Chapter 13

*J*ust before the holiday to Paris, I got a surprise in the post. It was a letter addressed to Miss Marie Jaffrey Smith postmarked Dunfermline. Dunfermline was unknown territory for me. I prised open the mysterious envelope and scanned the contents. The letter was signed by M Drummond, Principal, Dunfermline College of Hygiene and Physical Education.

I gasped as I read the content of the letter for a second and third time gradually realising that Miss Drummond was inviting me to go for an interview for a post of lecturer in the Games Department.

The vacant post would involve some lecturing for such subjects as Anatomy and Modern Studies which covered theory of dance.

The main thrust of the job would be teaching games and all types of sports including Hockey, Lacrosse and Netball. In this domain Miss Amer reigned supreme as Head of Department. The primary function of the post was to assist students to improve their personal performances as well as educating them in how to teach schoolchildren. Assessment of the students' ability to teach was central to this role.

I was shocked. After all I had only been out of college and a teacher myself for a total of two years. I was only just coming to terms with teaching children, far less students.

There was no way that I could contemplate accepting Miss Drummond's offer. It was flattering to be asked but realistically I felt that teaching students was a step too far – several steps too far at this stage.

The thought of having to make a decision ruled my life over the next few days. When in doubt of this magnitude I turned to Mum to discuss the matter.

We sat side by side in the car. Mum was adamant that I should go for the interview. She was keen that I should not be trapped in an all girls' school for my entire career, comfortable as this might feel at present.

I made up my mind to go, feeling that if nothing else the experience would be useful for the future and much as I might question it my mother was usually right.

Shortly after the interview I received a second letter offering me the post. After yet more discussion I accepted the job and with much sadness handed in my resignation.

On the appointed day Mum drove me to my new abode in Dunfermline. Whilst I was settling into Abbey Park Place Mum returned with a good luck present. The fabulous new handbag was just typical of my mother's generosity.

The following morning I examined my new timetable with my Head of Department Miss Amer and met Miss Wrightson, Head of the

Gymnastics and Miss Jarvis, Head of the Dance Department.

Lecturing on Anatomy was a daunting prospect but I was saved by the use of *'Gray's Anatomy'* on many an occasion.

Miss Amer gave her new member of staff a task that had to be completed every morning. She handed me a register. The students in each three college years were listed alphabetically. The Games register contained the detail of every position played in every sport and game for every student for each day.

This record keeping ensured that no student could complain that they had had insufficient experience in any sport! It was a boring and time consuming task but a useful safeguard for the college.

During that first week at College Miss Jarvis arranged the start of a community ballroom dancing class. To make up numbers I was required to participate. Five young men joined the class that night and they were to become lifelong friends. They were Douglas Weir, Cameron Goodall, Bert Rutherford, Fraser Shepherd and James Marshall.

A new social life arrived very quickly!

Change was a concept that Dunfermline College embraced. The College was sponsored by the Carnegie Trust and for student safety, being so close to Rosyth Dockyard, moved to Aberdeen for the war years.

I joined the staff at College in the first year of its return to Dunfermline.

However, no sooner had everyone settled than Miss Drummond decided that Aberdeen had much superior connections to academic facilities than Dunfermline. As a result the whole college moved back to Woolman Hill, an ex hospital in Aberdeen, at the start of my second year. It was at this time that the college lost its connection to the Carnegie Trust.

Our Principal was ambitious and even at this point in the College's history progress towards degree status for the Dunfermline courses was on the agenda.

Miss Drummond supervised everything about the remove. On one occasion whilst visiting the work completed in a student's residency she did not like the new stair carpet and despite the expense had it replaced immediately.

I was provided with free accommodation with the students. A colleague Margaret Rankin and I had the additional task of being 'advisers' to the students in their boarding house.

This was not an onerous task and much enjoyed by both of us. It was here that I found Miss Amer had another role for me to play. I became her driver under strict instruction not to exceed twenty five miles per hour and I will never forget the trip from Aberdeen to Edinburgh at that speed!

This was an exciting time for me, learning college ways, teaching students and enjoying all the fun of a new courtship with Douglas. Together we explored the byways of Aberdeenshire in Douglas's Vauxhall. It was in this car that I learned to drive and I took my test in it on a snowy day in the spring.

At the centre of my life, however, was playing hockey to international standard. I was selected to join the international side to tour South Africa and Dunfermline College were delighted to release me. This was indeed a feather in Dunfermline College's cap.

The tour of Southern Rhodesia was long in the planning and had begun whilst I was still at St Leonard's. It was essential that everyone helped to raise funds for the trip by running sales of work and coffee mornings. In retrospect publicity for the tour was poor and I'm sure we could have done more.

The tour took place in 1950 starting from Edinburgh on Thursday 1st June and not arriving back until 9th September. Travel to South Africa was by the Castle Line on the liner RMMV Warwick leaving from Southampton. There was only one stop in the ten-day sail. That was at Madeira. It was the same on the return journey.

There was plenty of room on board and a great deal of entertainment was on offer. The arrival at Cape Town topped by the distinctive Table Mountain was like entering a new world. There was a vociferous welcome from a college friend, Sheila, who was teaching in Johannesburg. That made the arrival all the more special. However there was little time to linger.

A long train lay alongside the Cape Town docks. It was to carry all eight teams and be our base for the length of our stay. The Scottish team found their niche, allocated their bunks and unpacked. It was similar to a British train except the seats of the daytime turned into beds for the night-time.

The route ran from the Cape through the lands of desert and

cultivation, the scenery changing from plateau to grasslands and hills. It finally crossed the border into Southern Rhodesia, aiming for Salisbury.

En route there were both scheduled and unscheduled stops. This allowed the local people to flock to the train. Often they brought small handmade gifts preceding other things for tourists to buy.

The train full of European women must have looked strange and ill placed as they took the opportunity to practise and run up and down the gravel on the side of the track. We had been confined on boat and train for long enough!

I learnt to play bridge, serious bridge too. The aim of the game was to win! At the end of the game friends had either been made or lost! Certainly I retained the ability to play reasonably well although not with enough skill to satisfy my various partners when I returned to the UK. Still, it was a good game to know about in spite of having to endure muttered comments such as, "Why on earth did you bid that? Idiot!!" I either had to endure the observation as an accurate view of my character or retaliate in kind complete with the 'look' and 'tone of voice' or withdraw and play no longer. I chose to grin and bear it. After all, I was a sitting duck. And I had learnt something!

Salisbury (Harare) in Southern Rhodesia (Zimbabwe) was the destination. It took three days to travel 7,000 miles to reach the match which would start our sequence of games. Our first match was against Ireland and to be played at Umtali, a town near Salisbury. It was a marvellous game and my team mates said that my goal had been a beauty from the edge of the circle. This was my contribution to a 3-1 win for Scotland.

Suddenly the 'real' tour had begun.

The weather was ideal – warm, but not too hot. The Scottish uniform was not designed for wear if the weather was hot: three-quarter length socks instead of stockings were allowed but tunics were still the order of the day. It made very hot work to play a full match.

At that time the line-up of eleven players on the field was fixed, i.e.:

Goal Keeper

Right Back, Left Back

Right Half, Centre Half, Left Half

Right Wing, Right Inner, Centre Forward Left Inner, Left Wing.

In other words:

1

2   3

4   5   6

7   8   9   10   11

I played in either centre forward or right wing position.

These were the fixed positions allocated to the eleven players. In addition there were two reserves. However no substitutions were allowed during the game so if someone was injured the team had to play on with only ten players.

What a great time it was! In all nineteen matches were played because besides the opposition from international sides we also played various Provincial teams whose lands we passed through by train.

This helped us to stay match fit. Everyone recognised that internationalists had to be 'fit' in order to play well. However, it was thought to be enough to leave exercise and training mainly in the hands of each individual player. Coaching sessions were few and far between.

The need for a formal coach may have been recognised as a gap in our preparation for competition but a traditional lack of speed in decision-making, taken together with the limited election of new people to influential posts in Scottish women's hockey circles, meant that changes did not happen. 'Hang on to power once you have found it!' was an essential mantra to the traditionalists and so, the selectors, five rug clad tartan ladies, held sway over every development within the game.

The organisation of international matches was usual but managing an international tour was real enterprise in those days.

Those taking on such a role were superb administrators but were not in any way expected to coach. It was not until 1972 that the traditionalists relented and I was appointed as Scotland's first coach.

It was at that point that Scotland began to catch up with the developments already implemented in other countries including England and the Netherlands.

But getting back to the tour. There was a judicial mix of matches and sight-seeing.

Salisbury was a pleasure. The Scottish team enjoyed the visits to famous places. We also left the train at various towns to stay in the homes of local people for a week or so.

It was a wonderful time with the exciting bite of international matches to keep our adrenalin levels high.

*

On one occasion I joined a group that went in a bus that wound up and round the road into the surrounding hills that led to the 'Leopard Rock' Hotel. There were no leopards to be seen on this trip. Alas!

Visits to tobacco farms and auctions, parks, gardens, diamonds and gold mines, all were included in a full and fascinating schedule.

To a girl coming from war battered Britain the towns and cities were stunning. We were taken to all the most prestigious places in Johannesburg – an amazing city, The Victoria Falls – indescribable beauty, Pretoria a magnificent capital, Stellenbosch – oldest country town, Port Elizabeth, East London, Queens Town – with rickshaws, Durban and Kimberley of the 'Big Hole' diamonds.

We were carefully steered away from poverty and apartheid and enjoyed our trip in complete ignorance of the politics of the country.

Time on the homeward journey passed quickly. There was always a deck game to join such as shove puck or badminton. There were no swimming pools on board in those days.

Waverley Station, Edinburgh was reached all too soon. The tour to South Africa was over and we were left with great memories and the strongest bonds of friendship. There was a strange affinity between the players. Nearly three months in a foreign country is often enough time to spend with people that you do not know well. But joining together to outwit and outplay opponents heightened the closeness, the dependency on each other. This was intensified as games were won or lost. Hockey is a team game and sharing the experience of a tour played at international level against opponents of like mind and skill surely laid the foundation for friendships that have lasted a lifetime.

Yet more exciting times lay ahead too. I thought I was harbouring a well-kept secret but I was somewhat naïve because it was written all over my face!

Chapter 14

Douglas! There he was amongst the welcoming crowd, waiting on the platform of Waverley Station, Edinburgh, on that dreary 9th September Saturday standing beside Mum, Dad and Drew. Scotland was a great place to be coming home to. Two and a half months was a long time to be away in spite of the almost daily letters Douglas and I had exchanged!

I laughed at myself as I remembered the letters. On board the mail was distributed on most days and there was nearly always one for Miss Jaffrey Smith. I took it quickly and swiftly propped it upright in the bedroom wardrobe beside a small picture of Douglas. My ever-changing room-mates had the wit to make no comment but it must have been pretty obvious that I was in love and Douglas was in love. It was a wonderful relationship, solid and sure and caring. Whilst I had been away Douglas spent his lonely evenings either playing canasta with his parents or making attractive rugs.

The very next day after I arrived home I met Douglas and we went to one of the best jewellers in Edinburgh to buy an engagement ring.

I was not a girl who liked to be covered in expensive jewellery but I knew the kind of ring I wanted on this occasion. This jeweller had plenty of choice so I had no difficulty in seeing what I liked. I slipped it on to my finger. It was sparkly and beautiful with a setting of two diamonds on a twisted stem.

"I'll never take it off," I whispered! Douglas just grinned. "I must go and show it to someone!" I said. I was so excited. "Let's go to see Auntie Nan. She'll love it!" Auntie Nan was delighted to be the first to congratulate us.

I have worn it from that day forward.

But that day was not the end of Douglas' surprises.

From Edinburgh we drove back to Crieff to tell Mum and Dad our news. Next we got 'properly dressed' and sped off to Gleneagles for a special dinner and dance with the band led by Henry Hall. The hotel provided a spectacular cake with a creative scene depicting a wedding sculpted on the flat top. And there was still more – a bouquet of pale pink roses. All these items threatened to overwhelm me. But the most precious thing I received that day was Douglas' unconditional love.

I returned from the hockey tour to be swamped by all the exciting events that were happening to me. Everyone was pleased about the love match.

It was September 1950 and there was so much to be done. First of all the wedding date was fixed. It was to be held on 17th August 1951 in St Michael's Church, Crieff. The Minister, Rev. Charles Hepburn, conducted the service. It was a medium sized affair with about 60 friends and relations attending.

I had been brought up in the Presbyterian Church of Scotland and had joined the church in Reading where the Rev. Vine admitted me to the church there. It would never have occurred to me to be married other than in a church. In the same way I would never have considered myself married had I been married by someone other than a minister.

It was exciting to choose my wedding dress and dresses for my two bridesmaids, and two train bearers. The tableau was completed by eight ushers and the bridegroom wearing the same tartan kilts.

I was very keen for Douglas to wear his kilt with the right stockings. I began to search for a pattern to knit these but despite extensive searching amongst all the patterns I possessed I could find nothing. Nevertheless I was determined that Douglas would wear the correct stockings. I put together several patterns and began to knit.

The evenings of my last term in the Dunfermline College Residence were filled with Douglas's wedding socks. They took a long time to finish but I was not overly pleased with the final result. I did not show them to Douglas and hid them away at the back of a drawer and was resigned to seeing my bridegroom dressed in the usual white stockings.

On my wedding day I walked up the aisle on Dad's shaking arm. He was more nervous than I was! My eyes dropped. I could not believe it! It totally distracted me. Douglas was wearing the knitted tartan stockings. I stared at them. They did look OK after all and I allowed myself to admit that they did complete Douglas's outfit. He looked so good. How happy we were going to be.

Our entourage of bridesmaids were Jean Sloan, Margaret Walker and flower girls Janet Butler and Jennifer Foy – from my 'second' families in Reading and Bedford respectively. They each looked very beautiful and collectively, they made a stunning picture. It was a gentle, sunny day; a good day for taking photographs. The reception venue was ideal. On loan for the day through the generosity of the Sturgeon family was Ochinflint House and grounds.

The reception was a simple but stylish affair. It was held in the dining room of the house. The meal on offer was afternoon tea. The wedding was timed for 2.30pm and the last guest left Ochinflint at 5pm. That was IT! Douglas and I left the house at about 4.55pm to go on our honeymoon. These arrangements were very much in keeping with the fashion and style of weddings of the day.

The afternoon tea comprised a fancy cake and a toast with the one alcoholic drink of the day. There was no choice of an alternative alcoholic drink. It was one small glass of wine or a glass of Robinsons orange juice.

Issues about having alcohol, or not, had arisen between Douglas and I when we got engaged. Mum and Dad came from non-drinking families and I, especially, had been well drilled in the need to keep it that way. I even told Douglas that I would not marry him unless he agreed there would be no drink in our house and that included the wedding reception. Douglas' family were much less stringent and enjoyed a social drink now and then, hence the compromise at the reception. It was many years before I relented and then we too enjoyed the occasional schooner of sherry or glass of wine

Our honeymoon was to be spent in Newquay. It seemed to be a good choice at the time but the reality turned out to be much more of an adventure than we had anticipated. We left Ochinflint in a decorated taxi to go to the outskirts of Crieff where Douglas' car was hidden. We were followed by a small group who wished us well with handfuls of confetti. We were heading for Northern England and the Border village of Abington via the single lane pot-holed road which was then the main road connecting Scotland with England. Douglas drove that night although as we continued south I became the main driver. The car was filled with our chatter about the day and how happy and successful it had been.

We joked too about another family difference of opinion. It was to do with the 'showing of presents'. Where to have that, Dunfermline or Crieff, or not at all! Such trivialities loomed large! During our drive we agreed that when we returned to Dunfermline we would acknowledge the need for both mothers to make this event a social occasion especially as friends and relations had been so generous. Douglas became all the more enthusiastic to support two 'showings' when he realised that in each house it would be an all female affair. He would not be required to attend!

I complained that I would not know half of those who came to the Dunfermline event. "All the better to have the chance to meet them before you are actually living in Dunfermline." The words sounded unsympathetic but the sentiment was softened by an arm round the shoulders and a kiss on the cheek. Douglas knew how to charm. I fell for it all the time.

However, the extended Weir family who had known him from birth tended to forget that time had passed and they still expected him to be at their beck and call despite his experiences since leaving school.

At 21 he was called up. He was made a 2nd Lieutenant and posted
to India for six years. After the War he returned to Edinburgh
University Dental College to finish his training as a Dentist. This
must have been very difficult to do after Army life during wartime.
When he qualified he joined his father in the family surgery.

Douglas worked very hard all his life. He was a popular and dedicated
dentist not least because he was interested in the lives of his patients
as much as in the health of their teeth.

One of the early impressions he made on me was a hardly noticeable
action but fully demonstrated his consideration for others. It
happened not long after we had met. Douglas had invited me to a ball,
a wonderful, full dress affair with every single man in a full dress
kilt outfit and every lady in a ball gown. I had gone with Mum to buy
one in McEwans in Perth. It was made of heavy satin, quite simple
with the skirt swinging magnificently from the waist. It was cut low
at the back. The front was shaped and a little risqué with just a hint
of tension to reveal the breasts of the wearer. It was a truly beautiful
creation. Mum and I were delighted with it. Douglas admired more
by the look in his eye than the words from his mouth. The two of
us had a great evening. The ball was an annual event and all our
friends in Dunfermline were there. The Glen Pavilion in Pittencreiff
Park was an attractive venue with a wonderful ballroom and we
danced the night away. This 1930s' Art Deco building has hosted
many a memorable dance since that night although Christmas party
nights are now perhaps a less glamorous replacement.

Like Cinderella all good things come to an end and the last waltz
drew to a close. Douglas and I fell into the music. We were both good
dancers and fitted well with each other. And the dress gave impetus

to the dance. We walked out of the Glen to reach the car. Douglas opened the car door; I gathered my dress to prevent it trailing in the dirt. That was to be expected but the 'extra mile' came on the return journey after Douglas had parked to help me out of the car. He got out of the driver's seat and ran round to the passenger's side. There, he opened the door again for me. How gallant was that?! It touched me as I could see what a kind, thoughtful chap he was. And from that day onwards he never ceased to prove it.

Douglas was always there in support of anything that I did

A walk down Dunfermline High Street with Douglas was an excursion too.

"Morning, Mr Weir."

"Who was that?" I would enquire.

"A patient!" he would reply. He was a favourite with everyone.

It's good to reminisce, now, where were we – ah! The honeymoon!

We had agreed to take two stops on the way to our final destination, one at Abington, that being a long enough journey to undertake from Crieff immediately after the wedding. The second stop was at Hereford on the evening of the following day.

We reached Abington about 8pm. 'Innocents abroad!' The 4-star hotel I had anticipated – Douglas, too, when he booked it – turned out to be the village pub, Scottish style! So the bedroom was totally unsuitable! The man in charge of this public bar was a shepherd lad by profession.

The place was very rough and ready but he did his best to help us and we finally found a bed in a guest house 'just up the road' (four miles up the road!).

Well after midnight we crawled into the narrow, hard three quarter size bed.

It had been some day for the new Mr and Mrs Douglas Weir!

That first day started an adventure that was to continue for decades.

The following day was hot, very hot. We made slow progress on the narrow roads of South West England to Hereford. So slow, in fact, it was late before we arrived at the hotel. Then on the last leg of our journey the weather began to change and the thunder and rain, monsoon style, burst out of the heavy black skies. Finally, we reached our hotel in Cornwall. It had been a long drive but we both looked forward to the next week where we could lie on the beach and sunbathe and just enjoy being with each other.

However that time was to be cut short. Instead of being away for ten days we agreed to return after a week. We were going to break our journey north at Liverpool.

Drew was about to sail to Southern Rhodesia and the newlyweds plus Dad and Mum were to foregather to see him off. It was not a happy affair. Drew was not yet twenty one and he was not at all sure if he should go or not. He had a job on a tobacco farm awaiting him. But anywhere in Africa seemed half the world away and I knew because I had been. Mum was understandably extremely upset and leant heavily on Dad's comforting support. And I had Douglas.

The newlyweds returned to Dunfermline somewhat serious-minded. But our new house, our new status as a married couple, as well as settling into a new routine of work and play was before us.

Lily and Marie, 1926

The Walker cousins, 1930

Smith Family, St Andrews, 1935

Marie at 21, 1947

Staff House, St Leonard's, 1947

1948, Training, Durban

England v Scotland, Oval, 1950

DCPE Staff and Yr 3, Aberdeen, 1951

Chapter 15

My first two years of married life in Dunfermline were busy. They were filled with activity, getting to know people whom Douglas had known all his life.

I resigned from College when I got married and although at that time married women were not expected to work I was offered a part-time job at Mary Erskine's School for Girls in Edinburgh. This was arranged with the head of PE there, Eileen Hyndman, who also captained the Scottish hockey side.

Teaching and hockey matches kept me fit. The 1951/2 international season had exciting possibilities with the fixture against England always being the most challenging. That game, for the first time, was to be played at Wembley Stadium in March. There was fierce competition to be selected. The five rug-wrapped selectors agreed on a final eleven, plus two reserves! I was to play centre forward again. Playing at Wembley was everyone's dream and I could not wait.

There had been a lead-in to the prestigious fixture, at Kennington Oval in 1950. Douglas, looking to become engaged then, had surprised me by flying down which was unheard of in those days! He appeared at the hotel where the Scottish team was in residence and then joined the crowds to watch the match.

He commented later that he was the only man in sight among 60,000 women!

The game versus England at Wembley was the same with over 60,000 screaming girls. I found the whole experience impressive. Going into the dressing rooms where so many famous footballers had changed. Coming out through the famous tunnel into a cauldron of noise – absolutely deafening! The game was disappointing as England won as usual, but it was quite an experience.

A break in the busy schedule came when Douglas and I went on holiday. We went to the Isle of Arran to stay in a guesthouse in Brodick.

Arran was a new adventure for both of us and we fell in love with the island. It was a love that lasted from that first visit to this very day. It truly is 'Scotland in miniature' with activities and facilities to suit all ages and tastes.

The ferry boat from Ardrossan was like a liner and the sail across to Brodick felt equal to a cruise.

This time away from everyone and everything was a great bit of peaceful interaction for both of us. The weather played its part too and the sun shone, the temperature rose, the guesthouse – only just affordable on Douglas' recently qualified dentist's salary – made it feel like a second honeymoon.

Douglas was employed as a general practitioner in his father's private dental practice. At the inception of the NHS in 1948 the three branches of dental practice, Private Practice, Local Authority delivered school service for pupils, pre school children, pregnant women and mothers of infants under one year old, and a hospital dental service were in their infancy.

A great deal of Douglas's work at that time was extractions often for young women about to get married. They and their families were keen to avoid the future cost of dentistry. A full extraction was often a wedding present.

However the start of the NHS dental service marked recognition that preventing tooth decay could improve the health of the nation. Never the less, in Scotland even by 1972, some 44 percent of the population over the age of 15 had no teeth. Finding ways to contribute to the new National Health Service as well as to continue to offer private service underpinned all of Douglas's professional life.

We were not rich but we were happy. We explored the island and found that the more we saw, the better it became. It was a reluctant drive back to Dunfermline.

Hockey re-commenced in the autumn of 1951 and the international season took off. I felt fit and well but my last game was against Belgium in 1952 at Ravelston on Scotland's best pitch surface. On that day I had a secret known only to myself.

I was pregnant!

However, a small blip at 12 weeks meant that I had to have at least an hour's rest every day and that was the end of my hockey playing career.

A rush of all sorts of emotions engulfed both Douglas and I.

Would it be a boy or a girl? Becoming parents, what a responsibility that was going to be! We agreed that there should be a 'family' name but also a name of the baby's own. So, after the baby was born she became 'Sally'. A beautiful, unexpectedly black haired baby girl! She bounced into this world four weeks early with the help of a pair of skilfully handled forceps.

That arrival changed the pattern of life for Douglas and I forever. The baby was the centre of all things and help was at hand from Mum. A fairly flexible routine was set up with fresh air and sleep slots carefully interwoven into the overall picture. The modern guidance on the best way to care for baby was to follow Dr Spock. I read avidly and incorporated his teachings into the children's welfare from that point onwards.

Needless to say we were besotted.

The Queen's Coronation was the great celebration for the country. TV sets were not common in many houses. Those who did have them found themselves entertaining friends for the whole day. Douglas and I were invited to Bert Rutherford's house. Sally, at six months, was invited as well. In strict accordance with the child rearing manual this was her first social outing and she loved it.

Auntie Nan invited Mum and Dad to her flat in Corstorphine to watch the Coronation on her TV. Auntie Nan was anxious for Mum to stay the night and return to Crieff the next day. Mum agreed but reluctantly. She and Dad were very seldom separated and she wanted to go home with him. However, he urged her to stay over and she did.

The following morning she got a message from Crieff to tell her that Joe had had a heart attack.

Douglas and I rushed to Crieff to see Dad. He was bed-ridden on the doctor's orders.

In those days the treatment for having a heart attack was to go to bed for at least two or three weeks. He was instructed to have no exertion, to move about slowly, to stay at home and do as little as possible. There was a suggestion that he should give up smoking but it was rest and treatment as an invalid that were the main strands for successful recuperation. Of course Dad did not return to work for nearly six months.

My focus of attention at this time was on Crieff and everyone reckoned that the car could drive itself along the road through Gleneagles.

Gradually, Dad improved and eventually he returned to work. He attended the cattle markets in Perth every Friday and he visited farms. I accompanied him whenever I could although I was pregnant again. Dad always said he had three women in his life: 'my wife and my wee wifie' and one yet to be named because he said he didn't know well enough yet (Sally).

It was 1955 which became a momentous year. Sally was two and a half years old. She attended a little Kindergarten class. This was the only one in existence in Dunfermline. It was held in a big old farmhouse on the road leading to Limekilns. She played there daily while everyone waited for the birth of 'her' baby.

It was a very hot summer and I followed my usual routine of a rest every afternoon to minimise the risk of miscarriage. Drew returned from Rhodesia and to celebrate Mum, Dad, Drew and I, with Sally, spent four nights in St Andrews.

July 1955 was an especially hot month but that did not stop everything going on as usual. That Friday 15th July Mum was supervising a tennis match with Miss Malcolm, Head of PE at Morrison's Academy. I had taken Sally for tea with Mrs Harper who was looking after her grandson Douglas, who was six months younger than Sally, and Dad, apparently fully recovered from his heart attack, went to the market held round the Old Kirk in the centre of Perth. In common with all the farmers who were there he was wearing his heavy winter jacket and warm jersey. The sun was beating down. The temperature was rising; Dad took ill and died.

The suddenness and unexpectedness came as a bitter shock to Mum and Drew and me. We had lost a husband and a father in one blow. It changed all our lives. Dad's death touched and changed many, many more lives than that of the direct family too and through the following decades I have continued to meet people who knew of and spoke very highly of my father.

Mum's family, Nan and the four brothers came to Crieff to help Douglas and Drew with the funeral arrangements, and to comfort Mum who was inconsolable.

I felt numb. I was concerned about the imminence of my second birth as well as my mother who was temporarily emotionally out of control. I turned to Auntie Nan. She was a rock for all three of us. She kept everyone steady. Not an easy task. The funeral director and the

Minister called to explain the procedures.

At that time only the men went to the cemetery for the burial. The women remained at home. Cremation might have been a possibility but it was not a traditional choice in the 1950s.

On the day of the funeral people began to arrive in the late morning. I kept very calm. The baby moved inside me almost sending out waves of comfort and sympathy. It was gentle little kicks that simply were reminders of the new life about to be born.

The funeral director gave the signal for the cortège to be assembled outside the house beside the mill. It was an appropriate start to Dad's last journey.

The people in cars joined in all the way to the cemetery in Perth. It was a big, big funeral.

Dad had been a popular figure in Perth and many people wanted to show their respect.

It seemed to me to be a very long time before the men eventually returned from Perth. In the house Auntie Nan involved the waiting women in food making, sandwiches, cakes and biscuits so that tea was ready when the men came back.

After the funeral there were many things to be seen to. Our main concern was about Mum. What was she going to do? Where was she going to live? How was she going to manage financially? These questions and many others only posed the need for more questions that required to be answered.

The immediate, short term answers turned out not to be so difficult to arrange. Drew also had a stake in the answers to the question of where to live. Drew had returned to Scotland six weeks before our father's death. He was indecisive about going back to Rhodesia and about the future direction of his life.

Mum could not remain in Crieff. Milnab House was a tithe house and belonged to Dad's employer Scottish Agricultural Industries (SAI). Mum had to vacate the house as soon as was reasonably possible and that she did. To begin with both Mum and Drew were welcomed by Douglas and I to stay with us in Garvock Hill until their future could become more settled.

Then I found a nice two bedroom flat in Cameron Street, Dunfermline and with financial help from her four very generous brothers Mum bought it. Mum managed and managed well Even getting a car. It was a tiny three-wheeled, two seater Bubble Car. This did not happen immediately and to begin with I took up the role of chauffeuse and ferried my mother across town to and from Cameron Street to Garvock Hill. The joyous event of 1955 for all of us came in late September. Robert Joseph Lindsay arrived, trouble-free into the Weir family. He was above average weight, with the fairest of fair hair which soon grew into angelic blond curls.

The new baby was a great distraction for Mum. She spent most of her time at the house in Garvock Hill. There, she helped to look after Sally and Lindsay. Her magical wee three wheeler Bubble car nicknamed 'The Little Soldier' becoming a great attraction for the children as they grew older. It was almost a child's car but could be persuaded to chunter along at a steady 35 to 45 miles per hour. It was an ideal town car and perfect for shopping and parking. It was not meant for touring the west coast of Scotland but it did with Drew as the driver and Mum the passenger.

The demise of this most useful and interesting car came about because of its structural frailty. Mum, with her usual show of determination and courage, drove it with aplomb in all weathers. This was especially so if the trip was to meet friends in Perth. One day in November she attempted the Glenfarg pass in snow and ice. Having a mind of its own the Little Soldier slid into a tree crumpling the front so badly the car was a write-off.

Fortunately Mum escaped with just shock and a few bruises. After that accident Mum bought a Mini, the fashion accessory of the 60s.

In Dunfermline I extended my range of friends which now included the wives of those young men who had attended that first dancing class. We met at each other's houses and encouraged and supported each other in running a wide variety of projects. This was a period of coffee mornings, raising money for charity, bringing up children and partaking in Church events. We often met up at the farm of one particular friend where a tennis court beckoned. We played tennis while the children had the freedom of a large garden and steading to play in.

I was also enjoying the thought of being pregnant again.

This time it was not just one but two babies on the way.

Twins were quite common in the Walker family. Auntie Nan had a twin sister, Janet, who sadly died from diphtheria aged two and a half. A generation before that Mum's mother had had a twin brother,

Tom but their mother died at their birth and the children were separated. Mum's mother, also called Lilias, was brought up in St Ninians, Stirling by 'Auntie'. Her brother Tom was brought up by an uncle who was a farmer in Crieff on a farm that is now owned by the Dron family.

Therefore when I told Mum she was not unfamiliar with the idea of having twins in the family. Nevertheless telling Douglas, when I returned from a pre-natal appointment and announced I had interesting 'news', was special.

"We're going to have twins! How about that?!"

Douglas took me in his arms. "Magnificent!" he said with rather a trembly voice. "I've always wanted twins!!" How brave was that!

Nine months in prospect seemed a long time to have to wait except in my case the time receded into its rightful pace because the medics had taken so long to find out there were two. They had become too big to be ignored. And they were born after only eight months.

The twins' birth came in the good order with Shona appearing first and Jaffrey arriving ten minutes later.

I was ecstatic. I could not get over having twins; one was wonderful but two was indescribable. They each weighed 6lbs.

My only discomfort during my pregnancy was a nasty taste in the mouth and some morning sickness which had never happened before. A cure for the morning sickness was offered by the doctor. I was against taking any pills, unless essential, especially while I was pregnant.

I have been grateful to the Lord for helping me to stick to that decision because that pill was the drug Thalidomide. There were dire results for those children and they often had to cope with severe handicaps from birth. Surely life is touch and go. But the birth of the twins, Shona and Jaffrey, made April 1958 very special.

Number 46 Garvock Hill was buzzing with children. There was Sally, aged 6 years, Lindsay, aged 3 years and then Jaffrey and Shona. The small house even managed to accommodate Drew when he needed a room after he had fallen and broken a leg playing tennis. He had been working in a Manchester bookshop but as a result of this injury had lost his job. Sickness benefit and keeping the job open for him was not expected in those days. Drew needed a bed for a while and joined us in Garvock Hill.

What a household!

A bigger house had become necessary to accommodate the growing family. An agreement was reached between Douglas and his parents to move into their house in Park Avenue. There was no discussion with me because it was simply viewed as the best and most sensible thing to do. And it was!

The move would be immediate. Mr Weir Senior would retire and Douglas would take over the ownership of the surgery.

Chapter 16

Number 16 Park Avenue was built in 1898 in the Victorian style, but it was designed to be more than a residence in its original usage. An extra wing had been added to the main block. This was to be used as a byre. It must have held two or three beasts, perhaps cows or horses, because the Deeds to the house included the right to graze cows on the adjacent park. When Douglas' father Robert Weir bought the house three rooms on the ground floor were converted into the dental surgery.

The young Weirs developed the business further. The byre was converted into two new surgeries and a waiting room with a toilet, thus freeing up all but one room in the main house. This turned out well in practice in spite of my fears that the children would interfere with the flow of patients. There were three entrances to the surgery with the children being banned from all of them unless escorted by an adult. This also gave the children freedom to use the large garden as a playground.

The move from Garvock Hill to Park Avenue was planned as a military exercise.

Changing the access to the surgery was a key priority and a new entrance was made through the extension to the surgery wing. This facilitated conversion of the surgery originally used by Douglas into a splendid new lounge looking onto the large garden. The waiting room became the living room-cum-dining room and was connected to the kitchen via a passage with a huge walk-in Butler's pantry. A further downstairs single storey wing housed a wash house, a scullery maid's bedroom and bathroom together with access to a cloakroom, large glass conservatory, tool shed and coal shed.

Upstairs mirrored the downstairs configuration providing four large double bedrooms, two with magnificent views across the river Forth to the Pentlands and two small single rooms. Above that was a secret stairway to a huge floored attic used for storing apples.

It was some house with an imposing front door which opened into a large hall with a broad staircase leading first to a half landing holding a long stained glass window then on to the top where the bedrooms were located.

The kitchen became the main centre of activity for the family. The kitchen faced the street at the front of the house. It was a naturally dark room but paint works wonders and the painter and I achieved that! The ceiling was painted in broad stripes of red and white. It brought the circus to Dunfermline!

Despite the new surgery there was still not enough room to house 'George, the dental technician'. Where was he to be housed? Of course! A wooden hut in the garden attached to the surgery wing on the garden side. Problem solved. Not only was that problem solved but an extra person was added to the child minder role. From the time of being toddlers and thereon until school took over, George was the main entertainer for Shona and Jaffrey. With his window wide open and his witches' brews bubbling away inside the hut the twins watched the production of crowns, bridges and sets of false teeth with wide-eyed wonderment.

It became obvious that some help would be needed to manage all the aspects of this new and more demanding life. Appearing like magic was Mrs Stevenson (Stevie). She had been cleaning the surgery for some time and agreed to add an hour or more to her morning times. In due course Mrs Leslie joined the team. The ladies split the workload of the surgery and the house between them. They were wonderful women who dedicated their working lives to the Weir family. They were married to miners and were neighbours who lived at the bottom of the town. Mrs Leslie had one daughter, Joyce, but that did not prevent her from spending her days at Park Avenue.

They both adored the children who had free run of the kitchen during the morning. They loved the dogs as well as the children and they were never ill. When Stevie retired Mrs Leslie took on everything.

She aimed to reach the surgery by 5am every morning. Even on Christmas morning she was adamant that she spend it at 16 Park Avenue.

Mrs Leslie had total charge of the kitchen where she produced the most delicious meals and baking. Her energy seemed endless and she became an essential part of the Weir family. She made her mark every morning at the gate leading into the surgery. There was a brass plate naming 'WEIR' to the world. The shine on that was her pride and joy and still acts as a memorial.

It took a while to settle into Park Avenue. Sally and Lindsay, in particular, missed their regular visits to retired neighbours Mrs

Whyte and her sisters the Miss Balds. They took a great interest in Lindsay, in particular.

Not able to drive themselves they hired chauffeur once a month. One day this included a visit to an appropriate pub that Lindsay loved to tell about – The Dander Inn and The Stagger Out.

'Helping' in their garden at Garvock Hill was a treat. In the summer there were all sorts of flowers and vegetables to pick. These retired teachers were wonderful and every Saturday Lindsay visited them. Mrs Whyte also had a good stamp collection so he learnt how to manage stamps. Lindsay missed these interests.

In the winter too, when there was snow, Sally missed going over the wall at the bottom of the short lawn at Garvock Hill. The dozens of houses subsequently built were not there at the time, only a rough grass field. She had the snow field all to herself but included some of her friends who lived down the hill. She was followed by Glen, the black and white collie dog.

I had always been accustomed to having a dog and when I got married Dad presented me with Glen. He was born on a farm and destined originally to be a sheep dog. He was intelligent and friendly. He was a caring dog too. One day he went missing from Garvock Hill and there was a great hue and cry to find him. He was found at a house at the other side of the hill, a little cottage where another dog of mixed breed lay happily in the sunshine. Glen lay close beside him. An old man was sitting on a wooden seat.

The man explained that the other dog was old and blind. Glen had discovered this and visited the old dog daily. Glen led the way and the old dog followed behind. So they went for a walk. Glen moved slowly to lead the way as they moved up the hill together. Yet he was very happy to return each day to his own family.

With the move to Park Avenue came another dog to fill the gap left when Glen died. Ruffy! Enter!

Ruffy arrived as a well-made cross breed puppy, Springer Spaniel and unknown black and white collie. His coat was white with a splash of black round the head by the ears and forehead. He had an average size of head and stood about three feet high. He had 'authority' indelibly written all through the cock of his head and the prick of his black, 'collie' ears. He could smile or frown at the person smoothing his soft straight coat. He stood square, at the ready to spring into action. He was on the go all the time and always looking for opportunities to engage in some kind of mischief... Although when confronted with possible misdemeanours he managed to look totally innocent as if butter wouldn't melt in his mouth.

At the front of Park Avenue stood an eight foot stone wall with a flat topped pillar at its end. It marked the boundary between the end of the property and the beginning of the public pavement and road. This wall belonged to Ruffy. It was his perch. From there he would survey, to the horizon, both sides of the pavements and road, across the front of the house and the entrances to the house and the surgery and, most extensive of all, across an adjacent road to a splendid big public park.

What a commanding position, as he saw it, his world. His favourite activity was to make use of these natural facilities. Ruffy would leap up on to the top of the wall in the back garden where it was not quite so high.

He strode along the top coping stones as sure-footed as any cat. When he reached the flat topped end he sat down. There he observed. If by any chance he spotted an alien, a foreign dog or cat, or bird, never a human being, he would give a push with his back legs, jump with his front legs to scramble down the face of the wall and bound across the obstacles in his way to claim his territory. His enemies always retreated. He hardly ever had to do more than glare at the intruder. That was enough to send them scurrying away. Ruffy would then wait to make sure they had really gone before returning to his station.

Ruffy set up another ploy. In the mornings after he was let out he went visiting. Many of the neighbours in Park Avenue had rolls delivered to their front door early in the morning, in time for breakfast. The Weirs had this service too. Ruffy became aware of all these lovely rolls in sites very accessible to him. He made use of his information by marking a trail to a certain area in the park. He hid the rolls he had collected under the bushes in his chosen area. Then he enjoyed eating them whenever he was hungry.

It took a great deal of detective work to really believe that it was our dog that was responsible! He was never caught actually stealing the rolls and he never, ever touched the large bag of rolls put in for number 16 Park Avenue! He was a great dog. He lived until he was twenty one years old. Dogs are said to be 'man's best friend' and in Ruffy's case that was true.

Park Avenue had a lot to offer the children. There was room in the garden to keep various animals, all of whom were characters. A very large white rabbit was master. One day he escaped from his hutch when Lindsay was cleaning him out. As luck would have it Ruffy was sunbathing. I heard the noises and went out to investigate. The circus was in full swing;

First the rabbit leading the field followed by the dog, followed by the boy. Round and round the garden they went, none of them quite catching another for a number of fast circuits. Finally Lindsay caught hold of Ruffy and the magic circle was broken. Everyone made sure that King Rabbit never escaped again.

Then there were parties. Sally and Lindsay were at the age for parties. There were football birthday parties for Lindsay and Halloween parties with fireworks and Christmas parties. I produced a Nativity Play for six Christmases in a row. About sixteen to twenty children were dropped off to rehearse every Saturday morning in December until Christmas. Then there were three or four performances. The 'theatre' that seated fifty people was the conservatory at Park Avenue. It was a great way to raise funds for Dr Barnardo's.

That conservatory had its good and bad aspects.

'Good' as a play room, 'bad' when first Sally and then Lindsay ran a hand through a glass pane in the door..

Lindsay's injury was more serious. He was being chased on the inside of the conservatory and ran straight at the glass squared door. His hand went through the pane but the injury occurred when he drew it back. The broken glass penetrated his upper arm and slit it wide open. Fortunately, Douglas was in the surgery next door. He bundled Lindsay into the car and took him straight to the hospital. There the injury was stitched up by the courtesy of seventy four stitches and the arm was put in a sling. Thereafter, Lindsay managed the 'wounded soldier' very effectively! Poor Lindsay!!

Picnics into the countryside combined with fires that would not light tried Douglas' patience and the small boys were sent to collect dry wood, in a soaking wet forest! None of them were Scouts; they were only as old as Cubs! Sally and her friends had never become Guides either so the prospect of boiled eggs for tea sank to nil. It rained that day so it was tidy up and home. The explorers' spirit wiped out!

The choir concert in the Carnegie Hall was much more successful. I collected choirs from all the secondary schools in Dunfermline. Each choir produced its own programme. Put altogether it produced an excellent, varied musical concert that raised a good sum to go to the ' Freedom from Hunger' campaign. This worldwide campaign of the late 1950s and early 1960s sought to contribute to alleviating starvation in developing countries.

With the same charity in mind our group of friends who met regularly, this time with Edith Robertson leading the way, met to plan and put together many favourite recipes to compile an unusual and easy cookery book named 'Freedom from Hunger'.

Taking action to secure improved living conditions for people both at home and abroad was gradually making a greater impact on our group of friends. As our children grew up over the next two decades we each found ways to continue to make our contributions.

Chapter 17

It was on a Wednesday morning that I took Sally, aged 8 years, to Edinburgh. We were heading for George Watson's Ladies College, George Square, Edinburgh. We were both nervous.

"Good luck!" I told Sally. "You'll be fine. I'll see you at lunchtime." We exchanged a kiss and I watched Sally walk into the school hall. The occasion was going to determine Sally's future. She was about to sit an entrance exam. Watson's had a good reputation. After all, my cousin Inglis had been dux of George Watson's boys' school in his day. His name is listed on the school board.

Sally was going into the lions' den not knowing what to expect. What she got was a whole day's worth of tests. Afterwards we took a tram along Princes Street, a sardine salad tea and a call into the news theatre for Pathe news and cartoons before going home made it a day to remember. Following a week's wait there was a positive result – she would attend Watson's School. She had done well.

She caught the two minutes past eight train everyday at the local station. A next-door senior girl took responsibility and escorted her to and from school. I watched her go every morning from my bedroom window and welcomed her back at varying times in the afternoon. These trains were full of school children attending a range of schools in Edinburgh. This meant that Sally had to get a bus or walk from

Waverley to reach the school. It was a testing journey but it did not appear to be dangerous. Giving such levels of independence at a young age was normal practice in those days.

There was no longer a kindergarten or Playgroup for the pre-school child to attend in Dunfermline. Instead Lindsay played with our friends' children the Robertsons with three children; Lamonts with two children; MacKinnons with two children; Shepherds with three children and others too.

The mothers of these families mostly had a qualification in their own right which they had used in some capacity before they got married but had not worked since. It was expected only that women have children and run a household. The only independent money that they received was the Child Allowance, after child number two was born.

These women occupied themselves and each other by running events to raise money to support charities. Of course their primary responsibility was for the children's well being.

The charities that I supported included Dr Barnardo's. I became the Chair of the Committee for raising money for the Dr Barnardo's residential house for children in the south of Dunfermline. I also drove round Fife distributing the little Dr Barnardo's 'houses' collecting boxes. Then every autumn I held a meeting when the boxes were gathered in and the money was counted.

Through contacts within Dr Barnardo's I learnt more about the issues and numbers of needy children in this country. It was through this work that I discovered an organisation based in York that was seeking families to host holidays for its needy children.

The main issues facing families included unemployment and family size which resulted in poverty and other health and social issues. Most of these children had never been beyond the end of their street, far less as far as Dunfermline was from York.

Both the parents and the children needed a break from each other. Through this organisation it was suggested that two small boys aged eight and nine from two different families should travel from York to Dunfermline to have two weeks' holiday as a member of the Weir family. Thus, Alex and Simon arrived. They had never been away from home before but neither of them showed any sign of home sickness and entered into a range of activities pursued by the Weirs with great enthusiasm.

The Weirs saw to it that the programme fitted in with their capabilities. Like little sponges they absorbed all that was new to them – and there were plenty of things that were new. So well integrated did they become that the holiday was repeated for three more years and direct contact was kept into adulthood.

The Weir family learnt a great deal from their friendship with Alex and Simon but although I kept in touch with the organisation no further opportunity arose to have more children on holiday.

Instead a struggling Dunfermline family came to my notice.

It was one Christmas week. Dr Barnardo's committee gave a party for the needy children of Dunfermline. I was one of the helpers. This was an occasion I enjoyed. I loved to see the children having a good time and doing things that they would not otherwise have the opportunity to do. The party was a huge success with the playing of party games such as 'Pass the Parcel', 'Oranges & Lemons', having cakes for tea and being taken home by car.

Except not all the cars stuck to their given schedule. One forlorn little family were left sitting together with anxious looks on their thin faces. Eventually this small group of three – Ben, aged eight, his sister May, aged six, and the smallest one, Joan, aged three – were all who remained.

I spoke to them to reassure them they would be collected soon. But time passed and no-one came.

"I'll run them home myself!" I decided and then bundled them into my car. The children went with me readily enough, relieved that something was being done to help them.

"Where do you live?" I asked the boy.

"My mam is in a cottage at Townhill."

"Very well." I drove off to travel the short distance. I went into the cottage with Ben. There I saw the poorest of poor furnishings in a grubby, small, smelly room. In it a girl (Anne), not much younger than Ben, sat on a hearth rug before an unlit open fire, holding a four month old, pale and unnaturally quiet baby. The room was cold. The mother of this struggling family was sitting on a wooden stool peeling potatoes into a cracked bowl which she held between her knees.

She looked up at me as I followed Ben into the cottage. Her skin, which should have been healthy, was drawn and grey with tiredness and stress.

Before she could speak I explained my unexpected presence. "Sorry to barge in, Mrs Hogg. It is Mrs Hogg, isn't it? I've brought Ben back. I'm sorry if we're later than you expected."

"Och aye." The woman acknowledged my comments with a nod of the head.

"It was a guid party," Ben told his mother but no-one was interested. The silence was awkward. So, I left with the idea of doing something positive to improve the Hoggs' living conditions if I could. The chance to do that came sooner than I expected. The very next day in fact.

I had made a list of essential jobs that were urgent to improving the Hoggs' cottage.

I noted electricity, fireplace, hot water, floor covering, cushions, table, clothes – the list could go on and on but I had only had time to notice and half guess what was needed. I needed a much more thorough examination, and upstairs in the one and a half bedrooms too.

What I had omitted from my list was outside, including the facilities for washing – both persons and clothes.

Despite this being the 1960s there was neither bathroom nor any running water in the house. Water had to be carried in to the living room and a tub filled with cold water was used for washing everybody. There was no such thing as modesty in these surroundings.

The 'steamie' for washing clothes was provided for in a self contained building at the end of the garden. These little stone huts were just big enough to contain one to four stone basins. There was just about enough room for the washer woman to squeeze in.. Underneath each basin was space to lay a small fire which heated the water. Once these were lit they burnt fiercely, quickly generating enough boiling water for the washing.

Setting up and using the 'steamie' was a weekly Monday performance. The 'steamie' was also a social meeting place and lots of gossip changed hands.

Women today have little idea of the manual labouring that their very recent predecessors had to endure.

In the case of the Hoggs, there was no longer a 'Mr' Hogg – they had no neighbours to offer help either. Neighbouring cottages had been knocked down and there were no people left in her street.

Hence the lad Ben, standing on the doorstep of 16 Park Avenue a few days later.

"An awful thing's happened. Mam doesn't know what tae do."

I took him inside the back door and heard his stuttering explanation. It transpired that being a Monday Mrs Hogg had decided to do a wash in the steamie. At the same time the baby was howling and demanding food. Ben had gone down the street to get a loaf of bread. One of the girls was chopping wood for the 'steamie' fire. That left the older girl, Anne, to sort out the washing and put them into the basin. The water had been heating up nicely and the water was almost at boiling point. The children were all absorbed in their various tasks.

With the baby guzzling his bottle there was peace and quiet.

Suddenly there was a flurry of movement followed by a screaming, heart-rending shriek then more loud shouts and yells.

"Mam, Mam." One by one the children appeared in the doorway. Their faces were white with fear. In the background there was a continuing noise of burbling water and more subdued groans and shouts.

In response Mrs Hogg rushed to the back door which was standing wide open. Arms were being flung about trying to get hold of something to help to lever the second daughter out of the boiling hot water that filled the 'steamie' basin.

Poor Anne was badly burnt but had some compensation and comfort in the knowledge that although some parts of her body had sustained horrific burns, her face had avoided being submerged and so she was not obviously disfigured. The accident did provide evidence of the dangers within the cottage though. I was able to use this incident in my subsequent drive to have this and other cottages removed and the Hoggs re-housed in a fairly new area of the town. It also gave me the opportunity to keep in contact with the Hoggs to try to contribute to raising their quality of life. It was a difficult period for Mrs Hogg although with the 'new' house some of the pressures were removed.

It took a long time for Anne's burns to heal but gradually she recovered. The other children entered school and Mrs Hogg was able to devote some time to the baby and the running of the household. Ben led the way when he left school at the age of 14 years. He became an apprentice in a Funeral Parlour and had a steady job there.

Eventually the whole family thrived.

Back to schooling for the Weirs. When Lindsay's turn came to go to a school in Edinburgh he too had to face a day's worth of tests and he was accepted by Melville College. Lindsay had been broken into schooling going to Commercial School as Sally had done. This was about a fifteen minute walk from Park Avenue. It took Lindsay a wee while to get used to having to go to school and it was a great help when the older boys discovered how good he was at football! That was his game although he was a very good all round games player.

His dedication to football was evident on a bright Saturday when the Round Table Association went for a picnic. There the men kicked a ball among themselves plus Lindsay, aged two and a half years. And, he did this the whole afternoon. The men were impressed!

Sending the children to private schools was a decision that Douglas and I made in the light of our own schooling experiences but we were determined that they would be day pupils not boarders.

Finding the cost of their schooling was a constant worry for Douglas especially as the way in which dentistry was funded was undergoing extreme change as the NHS determined the limitations to fees for services. Douglas was not at all convinced that it would improve dentistry but with some caution he followed the new rules. It was not long before the transfer to the new system was made and he worked very hard to be sure that his growing family were well looked after. Gradually the business expanded and an additional dentist joined the practice. When Douglas retired the practice was able to support four dentists.

Chapter 18

*A*t home, Sally was not happy. She said very little about her school and it became obvious that all was not well. At the end of the first school year we decided that a visit to the Headmistress was necessary. I made the appointment. Once at the school I was ushered into her presence.

She barely lifted her head to acknowledge me. She was constantly smoking and rude throughout the time we were together. However, following a further year we decided to withdraw Sally from the school.

Then there was the problem of which school would Sally attend for the rest of her education. Cranley School for Girls won the selection. Sally went to Cranley quite happily followed by her sister Shona when her time came. Both girls finished school with respectable exam results which enabled them to take their next steps into achieving higher education qualifications.

In the summer of 1960 we booked a house in Kingsbarns for a fortnight. Kingsbarns was a change from St Andrews and it was a momentous summer for Lindsay. This was the summer that he learned to ride a two wheeler bicycle and he practised and practised until he could do it perfectly. Shona and Jaffrey loved the rocky beach there. The twins searched for crabs and sea anemones in the rock pools. One day Shona was concentrating so hard on what was in the pool that she lost her balance and toppled face first into the water. Her face crumpled into tears as only Shona's could. Jaffrey, as an onlooker thought that it was done purely for his entertainment and doubled up with laughter.

Shona and Jaffrey were very good to each other. There were very few arguments or disagreements. It was the same with Sally and Lindsay. The four of them were usually in harmony and it seemed that the age gap between them was about right, wide enough not to interfere with the one sibling above or the one below. Of course having twins was helpful. Shona looked after Jaffrey's needs while he graciously accepted her good services.

The one time when they did disagree was on holiday in St Andrews. They were about 18 months old and used to having a pram each. This time they were in a twin pram facing each other. Neither enjoyed the experience!

Much later in life, when they were aged eight years, my college friend Sheila Thomson and I exchanged children to give them a holiday in each other's family. I put Shona and Jaffrey on the train at Waverley I armed them with a picnic accompanied by strict instructions not to open it up until they had passed Dunbar station.. Shona was put in charge of the food and drink and a lady in the carriage asked to 'watch' them. All was in place with Shona and Jaffrey sitting sedately in their seats. The train pulled out.

Apparently Jaffrey gave it about three minutes. He waited until the train had passed out of the Edinburgh suburbs before he leapt to his feet.

"I'm hungry!" he announced. "Let's see what Mum has given us to eat."

"No! No! Mum said we couldn't eat until we had passed Dunbar! We're only out of Edinburgh! You sit down. You'll just have to wait!"

The debate over we're not eating yet! Shona pulled rank, having been born ten minutes earlier than her twin.

Sometimes he was difficult for her to control. Their understanding of rights and wrongs did not always tally. However, this time she was determined her brother would behave. It was such an exciting venture she was determined to do the right thing and keep to the rules.

Douglas and I were quite aware of Jaffrey's dependency on his sister. Being boy and girl made it easier as they had different interests and of course wore different clothes.

Clothes were a bone of contention because I was very keen on kilts – the children were not so enthusiastic about wearing them, especially when they first went to school, at Commercial.

Kilts were expensive so although I was no expert seamstress, I decided to make a kilt each for the twins. I went to a 'proper' tartan shop and chose the Anderson tartan because it had a nice colour of blue within its spectrum. The offshoot of the Weir clan was the MacPherson, the tartan that was correct, but it was 'too 'red' for a child's tartan. So the length of the Anderson tartan was made up into two little kilts held up by ill-fitting white bodices. Shona and Jaffrey complied patiently and without protest – Mummy said they were to wear the kilt, so they did! Only much later did they tell of their unhappiness at obeying orders. Still, Shona and Jaffrey survived.

As babies growing into toddlers and integrating with Sally and Lindsay the whole family was a joy.

Lindsay had re-christened his grandmother although no-one could guess the origin of the one he chose to call her. She was very happy with it. Everyone called her by it. How was it spelt? The Reader can decide but whatever the choice it must be admitted to be original! Do-De-Do-Do-OO-Do-Do-De….. It was a monotonous rhythm and he soon fell asleep, and hence forward everyone called her Do. It suited her – Do. It characterised her 'young' qualities without undermining her ability to make friends with all ages.

The summer of 1961 was fraught with many happenings including more good news.

In the beginning of the year I announced that I was pregnant again. Baby No. 5 was on the way! I followed my usual routine of taking a rest on my bed.

Chapter 19

*H*olidays were relatively few and far between although both Douglas and I subscribed to the need for at least one per year.

When Shona and Jaffrey were two and weaned from the bottle and breast respectively I was keen to have two or three nights away by myself. This was something of an impossibility at Park Avenue! I had enrolled onto a course in creative writing and I was very anxious to complete this. Douglas gave his full support, as he did in every project I wanted to pursue, and there were quite a few over the years!

I also enlisted Mum's help and as usual she supported me in every way she could. I was extremely blessed in all that I did because the people round me straightened the way ahead with such skill and dedication. It was this that made it possible for me to attempt new challenges.

In this case I thought a hotel in St Andrews would fit the bill.

So, with some trepidation I went to the hotel in St Andrews. I had a nice room. For the first time in years I was alone. The two days that followed were perfect; the very best of St Andrews' weather with no wind and really hot. After breakfast I went to the Castle and claimed a private site. For the first time I had the space and solitude to begin writing again. This was a first attempt at producing a short story. My goal was to submit the story to the People's Friend. Whilst this first attempt was unsuccessful the very positive feedback that I received from the editor meant that I kept trying and over the next 20 years the People's Friend accepted some six stories for the magazine and a further two for publication in their Christmas Annual 1988. Having two stories included in one publication also meant the invention of a pseudonym, one of which was Shona Jaffrey. In those days the reward for having a story published was £100 and a People's Friend tea towel!

At home Mum was busily directing the household traffic with the tentative assistance of Auntie Torrie (Jean Torrance, a long standing hockey friend). She had volunteered to 'help' without knowing exactly what it might entail! However, the children enjoyed it and thought they'd been "good"!!

Holidays matched the cycle of the educational year. At the beginning there was Sally, with slightly longer holidays of a fee paying school. Shona went to Cranley School for Girls following Sally's footsteps. Jaffrey followed Lindsay to Melville College.

My final pregnancy resulted in Gavin Peter Weir. He was three weeks early, weighing in at 7lb 12oz and he entered the world active and ready to have a go at anything. He was an exceptionally 'good' baby and thoroughly enjoyed the attention of his siblings. My brood of five gave Douglas and I great joy – and that is not just saying so in retrospect!

Gavin's birthday was in April, the day after Shona and Jaffrey. It was also Mum and Douglas's birthday month too.

By the time we reached August that year we were all ready for a holiday.

Up until now we had holidays in St Andrews or Kingsbarns because all the children needed was the sea and sand, with an added wall to jump on and off.

Those early holidays in St Andrews were a repeat of my own childhood holidays when we were taken by Mum and Dad. We had always had a great time and one event often retold by Mum highlighted the small open-air theatre on the way to the outdoor swimming pool and beach that was given over to the children's entertainment. Various 'events' took place on its stage. A competition was run to find the most entertaining children's 'act'.

One day Mum turned the corner to be faced with her two children on centre stage! We were standing side by side and singing, in tune, one of her songs: 'When I went to the Zoo'.

We looked a likely pair according to Mum. The passing audience evidently thought so too as we were voted winners of the competition.

However, much as we loved going to St Andrews, Douglas and I had decided on a change.

We decided to try a different venue, not far from home but offering new facilities. We booked a house in South Street, Elie and rented for a month with Douglas joining everyone for two weeks and at weekends.

The front door opened yards from the sandy shore overlooking the bay and the harbour. It also had a back garden which was ideal for putting baby Gavin in his pram for his sleeping times. It was also easily accessible as a change from the sea-front. It lent itself to the older two as they became involved with an organisation that had a profound influence on the Weir summer holidays for the next thirteen years.

The Children's Special Seaside Mission (CSSM) was, and had been, in place for some years previously, organised and funded by the Scripture Union. The CSSM reminded me of my own childhood and my introduction to Christianity through Sunday School and Crusaders in Reading.

Eventually all five Weirs joined the CSSM in their various age groups and took part in everything on offer from Sally, and a little later Lindsay, becoming in their time members of the team when our holidays moved from Elie to Arran. All the girls on the team had to take their turn at cooking and Sally found it a demanding experience – no one will forget her queen of puddings! In his final year in Arran Lindsay conducted the service in the small Church that overlooked the playing fields at Whiting Bay.

Shona, Jaffrey and, a little later, Gavin, rushed down to the beach early every day to help to build and decorate a sand pulpit to be used later in the morning for the service and chorus singing that took place daily.

It was a sign of the times that a generation later there were so many rules and regulations in line with Health & Safety to 'protect' children that it was almost not worth trying to build a sandcastle, never mind a pulpit! Some traditions have held fast through the years though.

There are always two teams with current titles and the children all compete to win points for their team by undertaking tasks or memorising verses from the Bible and there continues to be an annual parent versus children sports activity of some sort even if less energetic than puddox!

In the 1960-70s there was freedom to use the team's own discretion regarding suitable activities. Games including puddox, Lindsay's best game, cricket and the 'wide games', at which Jaffrey excelled, occupied parents and older children and satisfied the teenage competitive spirit. Everyone engaged in the sausage sizzles and the happy soakings of building the hardiest sandcastle against the tide team fun.

And the evenings were filled with talking. The questions about life, and death, surfaced and led to many youngsters coming to a deeper understanding of religious principles and the life of Jesus Christ.. When we got home this was supported by going to church as a family every Sunday.

All in all there cannot be a more significant place to have the benefits of both children throughout the daytime and an equally enchanting peaceful location of scenic Arran in the evenings.

Arran also became the perfect backdrop for me to continue my writing. Indeed one of the published short stories is based on people meeting together on the Caledonia ferry.

Both Douglas and I had fallen in love with the island on our first holiday as a married couple in Brodick. Family holidays started based in Lamlash, moving on to Whiting Bay when this became the only village continuing to offer the CSSM. That special 99 ice-cream cone and 'I love Arran' became the icon and motto for the Weirs' summer holiday.

It did not matter what the weather was like on these holidays. If there was rain it never prevented the planned events going ahead although only once did Douglas brave driving us all round the entire island in the wet!

Arran offered us all sorts of age appropriate opportunities including making friendships which even now are still renewed at each visit. We had so much fun as well as some religious learning.

The holiday began as soon as we stepped onto the Caledonian ferry boat in Ardrossan. Given reasonable weather the beach was the place to meet; family groups holidayed year upon year, renting the same house or trying out a new one and soaking in the uniqueness of the island. I even managed to knit Norwegian patterned jerseys while ensconced on a chair basking in the sun behind a canvas shelter. Every summer the family had a jersey each all knitted with the same background colour to be easily identified. Going home was always hard but our car load was always well entertained and Sally and Gavin made up funny conversations. Gavin was a 'wee comic' and his phrase "a healthy smell" is still quoted today.

Chapter 20

*I*f Arran was the Weirs' summer holiday place we also had a weekend land-locked retreat much nearer Dunfermline. THE COTTAGE!

Douglas and I had always dreamt of having a country retreat. We were lucky enough to notice one for sale about three miles from the village of Saline, itself nearly six or seven miles from Dunfermline.

Impatient as ever, I wanted to view it immediately. I thought the house sounded attractive and suitable. So, the two of us set out to assess it.

The cottage was positioned on a small hillock on the end of a farm road on the back road to Saline. The stone built Scottish style of the early 19th century cottage was beautiful, with views all round it equally magnificent. The central long distance view stretched as far as the eye could see. It ran westwards on and on to the Wallace Monument in Stirling and along the base of the string of the Ochil Hills. With the sun shining from the west the detail of the landscape was a delight. 'Spectacular' was an inadequate description of such a God-painted picture. What could the inside be like to attempt to match or even complement such a background? Douglas and I slid the old fashioned heavy lead key into the well-worn lock on the front door.

Originally built for a resident game-keeper, the cottage had four primary rooms. The living room with a fireplace had windows that faced the front and had the splendid views. Directly behind this was the larger of the two bedrooms.

The other front room on the left of the front door was the kitchen and behind that was another bedroom. At the back in between the two bedrooms was a tiny box room.

Our immediate reaction was mutual. It would be an ideal holiday cottage if a few extra touches were added here and there.

After all, essentials would have to be put into place including a toilet into the box room together with running water in both the new bathroom and the kitchen.

But before any alterations could be put in place, the Cottage had to be bought. The asking price was £1,000. I wanted Douglas to put in an offer there and then but he, always more cautious than me, suggested we 'sleep' on it. My gut feeling was that as it was such an attractive buy it would not be long on the market. But how important would one more night be?

By the next morning, early, I could not get to the phone quickly enough to put in our offer. I could not believe the reply!

'Sorry! It was sold last night. An offer was made and the deal done before midnight. Sorry about that!"

I handed the house phone to Douglas to try to undermine the offer accepted by upping ours. The seller would have none of it and just kept on repeating "The deal is done!".

Then we had an unexpected call. The chap who had bought the cottage contacted us and said, "Tell you what, when we sell the place next time round we promise to give you the first refusal? Then you can have the best chance of buying it before anyone else comes along. How about that?"

"Half of a reprieve!" I muttered.

"Better than nothing and all alterations may be completed by then." Within the year the cottage was once again on the market and Douglas and I sealed the deal after submitting a bid offering a further £50.00. In that time only running water and electricity had been installed

The driveway to the front entrance had been re-laid although the farmer's tractors roughened it up pretty quickly.

Douglas and I only installed basic furniture. The four sets of bunk beds were reclaimed from the Royal Navy shipyards at Rosyth and were the perfect size for the children and their friends – boys in one room and girls in the other and Douglas and I on a fold out bed in the sitting room.

The easy, quick access from Dunfermline was the greatest asset because the family could be taken for an afternoon or go there for a week with the option of returning to Park Avenue if necessary. It allowed the children, and the dogs, total freedom to run wild and to do things that only country-bred children can do.

That was where Jaffrey learnt to drive a car. There were several cars of different shapes and sizes available to those in the family who could drive or who were learning to drive.

There was a favourite, a very old, small blue van that stood up manfully to the battering it took, especially from Jaffrey aged 13. He mastered the art of driving very quickly and had a high-old time racing up and down the cottage track and adjacent field.

The cottage offered action, peace, beauty and, relaxation for all the family, with ages ranging from Sally's teenage years to Gavin's six years; from Douglas' enjoyment of his family to Marie's total absorption in writing and included Mum's ability to be with her family in space and light to sew her wonderful tapestries.

One of the first tasks, and there were many to follow, was to paint the whole cottage white! What a difference that made, especially in the spring when the cherry trees lining the entrance to the drive were in bloom.

Cherry Tree Cottage was forever a dream come true indeed. The workload did not lessen. The property had to be kept up to scratch so it was constantly under review by Douglas. He had a favourite job which followed him wherever he went!

He just loved to move stones. The wall was never in the right place, the right length, width, height, too many stones, too few, too flat, too round and so on! The stones could not be moved by Douglas on his own so the boys became his slave team. How better to harness the strengths of teenage boys? It was the perfect answer and what wonderful walls protected our perimeter.

One son was more expert than the other two so he was relied on to 'help' Dad with the stones. And he remained a specialist 'Stone Shifter'. His name is Jaffrey!

The rest of the family, and any of Sally's visiting boyfriends, were drafted into the working squad when the stones became unmanageable. There were plenty of other jobs to be done every week as well as holidaying. In the back garden there were half a dozen prolific gooseberry bushes that were waiting to be picked and they made tasty jam!

Then there was 'Little Man'. The field in front of the cottage belonged to the farmer and he allowed it to be used to keep a pony.

One day tragedy struck.

As usual, on a lovely Sunday afternoon most of the family went to the cottage. When they looked there was no sign of Sally's pony. There was a worry about his whereabouts.

"Spread out and find him," I instructed. "He can't be far away."

He was easily found.

"He's here!" Gavin shouted within minutes. The boy rushed back to the cottage. He was very upset. Douglas went to investigate. Unfortunately the pony was dead.

The handsome 14.2 hand pony was behind a clump of mixed bushes. Sadly something in the bush turned out to be poisonous and had not been spotted by the farmer or us in time.

The cottage was always in need of painting. I took on the job of head painter. It pleased me to see the outside painted white leaving the outline of the windows and single entrance door painted a glossy black.

There was not enough room to house everyone comfortably in the sitting room so a rectangular sun parlour was added across the full front of the cottage.

This extra sunny room was helpful. It added space for Mum to sit with her tapestry and for Gavin to listen to a story read to him by her. I, too, did reading and writing while sitting in these inspirational surroundings. It was only later when the cottage was being prepared for our retirement that we thought to incorporate the adjacent byre.

A little bit of heaven on earth. There was even a stream across the end of the field where, if you were lucky, some frogspawn could be found. Then, it was tea-time and back to Dunfermline and the Sunday treat, fish or haggis suppers picked up from the traditional chip shop, providing seven steaming packages. Delicious!

The family developed rapidly through the 60s with my involvement in each of their schools and their individual interests and workload. I was particularly interested in the developments taking place in football and visualised how it could be adapted to improve the game of hockey. There was limited TV to allow followers of football matches to keep up to date and I missed going to the Saturday games with Douglas. However, we substituted this by taking Lindsay and Sally to play for their respective teams. Sally captained her University team. Lindsay, too good at all games, captained the school's rugby, cricket and golf teams. His great love was football which meant he played rugby in the morning and junior men's football in the afternoon, ferried throughout the day by his mother!

It was soon the turn of the remaining three, and so the taxi service continued. Jaffrey was a Scottish School boy hockey internationalist, while Gavin was an athlete running at Meadowbank. His school hurdles record breaking time remained unbroken for many years until the 1990s.

During those years I was contacted regularly by Eileen Hyndman. She continued to be head of the PE department at Mary Erskine School for Girls. We were both keen to obtain more publicity to promote hockey within the sporting world and to the public. We both thought that the Press could do more so we went to see the Sports Editor of The Scotsman. The net result was an invitation to write a column for The Scotsman every week. This was to be a comments column not a match description.

"You can do that?" Eileen turned to me.

I was not at all sure that I could but I took it on!

I wrote a column for The Scotsman for ten years and enjoyed doing it. This task kept me closely in touch with the hockey scene so I was able to hone my ideas in team management, team coaching and correct diets for the players. I was able to develop my ideas about tactics, in particular the use of player skills and movement through a game. I was also able to explore the importance of more interaction between players on the pitch, and getting to know each other off the pitch. (See *Women's Hockey in the 70s,*.) There was an excitement building about the application of these essential changes, although not all those with power in the Hockey Associations were in favour. In those days change was not easily embraced and it was an uphill struggle to engender belief that the risk would be well worth the angst and could prove successful. Those who dare will succeed. In women's hockey there was a pool of interested, active, enterprising young players who were willing to try out new ideas to reach a higher standard and win more games. They worked hard to match the demands of the first international coach Scotland had appointed. I became that very first coach.

It came about unexpectedly: an official letter arrived one morning. Would Mrs Marie Weir like to accept the position of coach to the Scottish International and Reserve teams for the following season?

What an offer? What an opportunity! Of course I would like to accept. This was a moment of decision making that was never in question. The possibility of putting into practice and trying out different ways of conquering other teams was irresistible. Scotland had never won as often as they should or could have done based on the skills that the players showed. To date there had been no concentrated and consistent effort to make the best winning difference. The gauntlet had been thrown down. What a challenge and with a great group of players. Although I had not met these players I had reported on their skills through my weekly column in The Scotsman.

The big moment of euphoria passed. Of course I could not accept the job. Guilt flooded through me. First of all there was Douglas. I knew, although I had not seen any timetable, that other logistical preparations for the fast approaching IFWHA Conference in 1975 were already in full swing. Taking on the task of coaching the Scottish team would inevitably take a lot of time, effort, a commitment and dedication that meant all other life would come to a standstill. That is, as I would do it because it would have to be all or nothing.

No, it was an impossible thing to undertake. Nice to be asked.

Devastating to have to refuse. But at the end of the day the family would come first and hockey was only a game.

Chapter 21

'**O**nly a game' was threatening to dominate the Weir household for a good part of the next four years. Everyone inevitably became involved in some way. That first invitation was thrust into Douglas' hand for his verdict, 'Yes' or 'No'. I waited.

"What do you think?" I asked as casually as possible.

"No…it is what you think." Douglas had analysed the dilemmas with pin-point accuracy.

Silence fell. Douglas put his arm round me. "You take it. The family will all be there and with all that support the Scottish team will never have won so many matches! England, here we come! How about that?"

Douglas was being his usual caring, thoughtful self. He knew his wife pretty well and in all situations like this he supported rather than blocked any enterprise I wanted to do. He could see what great satisfaction there would be in being the first coach of this promising group of players. "Yes" was the answer backed up by five other "Yeses" as the Weir family offered their support to the first Scottish coach!

Fortunately, the whole family were interested. Their after-match discussions were always full of constructive comments.

From my perspective that first coaching weekend was meeting with the players selected by the Scottish Women's Hockey Association (SWHA) selectors. The venue was to be the relatively new sports centre at Inverclyde. It was all new to me and to a number of the players.

I could not sleep long that night.

I drew the curtains and was greeted by a dramatic scene all dressed in pure white. A thick fall of snow had arrived during the night and had blanketed the several hockey pitches and the surrounding previously green patches.

My heart sank. How could I carry out the carefully planned training and practices that required dry, clear grass surfaces to make them effective? Not only that but the players themselves would find being outside in such low temperatures miserable. What a beginning to building a good relationship between me and the girls. I looked out of the window anxious to find some signs of relief. I could find none.

And I still had to meet the players. The sooner, the better.

The group of players had assembled in a windowless bare room. I guessed there must have been about fifteen to twenty girls, all sitting squashed round a table or leaning against each other on the wooden floor. There was a great background rumbling noise coming from the clashing of the conversations. A wall of silence fell in the room as I entered.

I scanned the upturned faces, searching for one that might be familiar. There was only one. Helen Flockhart, the Scottish goalkeeper and current team captain. I recognised her from my own playing days when Helen had been a young goalkeeper showing the potential that was in this instance being fulfilled.

Helen caught my eye and smiled encouragingly. I began my well rehearsed opening introduction and the weekend began. This was the first of many pre-match coaching week-ends.

It was cold and wet but out we went to show any doubters that in future training would be an all-weather activity and we regularly got wet three times a day! That first training session gave a taste of what lay ahead.

I prepared for the next morning's exertions so an order was relayed to the players – 'In bed by 10pm'. I learnt much later that the curfew was broken in a few instances but they always turned up on time the next morning!

A new regime was being put into place. The players seemed to like it. They responded with enthusiasm and were willing, indeed keen to absorb different techniques and approaches.

The big event in which I had taken part was to be included in the Scottish team selected to play against England at Wembley in 1950. As the Scottish coach the immediate 'big' event was still to play England, at Wembley and to win in 1972.

I had introduced different tactics this time. I had studied the leading football teams and spent a month with Laurie Cunningham at Falkirk Football Club to learn about fluid methods of play. I also joined a football coaching course at Stirling University as the only woman!

These experiences and the knowledge gained helped me to better understand how to win more often.

The day came and the Scottish team bus moved towards Wembley in unison with hundreds of other buses travelling from as far as Aberdeen in the North and Cornwall in the South. The air was full of singing supportive songs and waving St Andrew's flag. The level of excitement in the team bus rose and rose. This was something the players had not experienced before. What it was to receive V.I.P. treatment. Even a taste of it was sweet and motivating. For me there was a feeling of déjà vu because I had played at Wembley before. The bus arrived at the back of the Wembley complex and the players were guided to the famous dressing rooms. The interior of the dressing rooms had been improved since I had played there but they were still not luxurious.

The girls changed, then waited. This was the most difficult part of playing in any match...the waiting for the activities to happen.

At last the signal came. The team lined up. I made my way to the official seats in the stand. I had done all I could do with the players. Now it was up to them.

I walked through the tunnel to reach my seat on the edge of the pitch. I was not prepared for the volume of noise that hit me as I emerged from the tunnel. I had not remembered how overwhelming it could be to have 65,000 young, mostly female, voices raised in singing.

The preliminaries of presentation and exchange of banners duly completed, the players fanned out to go to their respective places on the pitch. I was nervous. The new tactics were in place for the first time. Would they work?

The tactics were quite simple but they changed the game, as they were intended to do.

England had been the most successful team worldwide for forty years. To them Scotland should be easy to beat as usual. They expected this match to be a walkover. Their every movement oozed confidence. They did have good players. Their star player was their left inner, Val Robinson. She had mastered the knack of scoring vital goals at just the right time. The team members around her played to her strengths and she produced the results that won the matches.

Of course, England played in the traditional formation. This was how hockey was played. I wanted to change this as did my players. My tactics put the players in different positions on the field.

There were two major changes in the Scottish approach. Instead of the players sticking firmly to their own parallel channel of activity on the pitch they were encouraged to move more freely in all directions in order to find or make space for themselves or for another better placed team member.

The other innovation was to delegate one of the Scottish team to man-mark the star forward in the English team. She, Margo Barr, was instructed to mark the Left Inner out of the game. This worked like a dream. It spiked the English guns completely. They had never been subjected to such nullifying tactics and they did not know how to cope with them.

Two goals by one of Scotland's star forwards, Mariette Craigie, roaming at her leisure, gave Scotland a 2-1 victory. Great rejoicing!

There is nothing like being a member of a winning team, especially a win that has taken forty years to achieve! The bonding between team members remains forever. That shared experience makes a strong, irreplaceable link. And many of the thirteen or so in the squad of 1972 are still in touch with each other today.

As the coach I was privileged to share some of their achievement and satisfaction. The English supporters did not appreciate the changes Scotland had introduced. They found it hard to believe the match had been lost. That evening the Scottish entourage were taken to the theatre – 'Annie get your Gun', a marvellous musical. It was a good idea and made a change from the usual after match dinner.

What a journey home it was on the train from King's Cross to the Waverley Station at the east end of Princes Street in Edinburgh.

The whole train was celebrating! How could they not join in with the strains of the hockey song as it reverberated from one end of the train to the other?

"Purple is the colour
Hockey is the game
We're all together
And winning is our aim."

And the girls had done it! The 'dream' team went even further, if anything could top the elation of Wembley, a draw with Ireland and a sound win against Wales meant Scotland won the Triple Crown that year.

Preparation had also begun for the 1975 World Tournament which would be hosted by Scotland in Edinburgh. But time was short, too short to incorporate new methods of play down to club and regional levels. A start had been made at the grassroots and clubs and schools were interested. Eileen Hyndman had been elected as the Scottish and IFWHA President, and she was primary supporter of our new methods. She did a marvellous job in promoting and consolidating change to produce a modern, faster, better game to play and watch. It was a marathon task but the players were keen to push ahead on the pitch.

These were the early days of seeking to change the role and responsibilities of the position of the coach. At this time only an appointed group of selectors were allowed to pick the international squad. In 1975 the player pool only consisted of 11 players and two reserves, not the squad of 15 or more that now exists. These selection methods limited my scope to apply a full range of tactics matched to the nature of each opposition.

However, the impact of the surprise of our new tactics ensured that our winning ways continued with more matches in the public eye. The opening game between Scotland and Canada at the World Tournament at Meadowbank, Edinburgh in 1975 resulted in a victory for Scotland.

I resigned as national coach after this tournament and accepted an invitation to go to Virginia to coach at a youth camp. It was an opportunity to visit the USA, and Anne Wilson from the national side and I went together.

When I returned I was offered and enthusiastically went on to take up the role of the official coach to the newly formed Scottish Schoolgirls' Association. I took up the baton of change with this younger cohort where the officials gave me their full support to increase the size and skill range of the squad and so secure a more tactical approach for each international game. The players came straight from school teams where they emerged playing the traditional game but very open to change.

It has taken time and a lot of effort to radically change the game of hockey. Most of the changes have been welcome and have enabled more creative play. Players have been more fully engaged in shaping tactics, enabling them to be more confident and skilful in tackling the opposition effectively.

Publicity has not been Scottish Hockey's greatest asset in spite of the men and women's Associations joining up into one body, the Scottish Hockey Association in June 1989.

The public's interest was being poached by the huge growth of the Scottish Ladies Football Association.

Television has mostly passed by Scottish Hockey. The Hockey administrators would do well to review their publicity strategies and adjust them accordingly. It is such an exciting game to watch as well as play that it would be good to see it gain a more prominent position within today's sporting spectrum.

I resigned from my post as the Scottish Schoolgirls' Coach, having supported a number of girls to progress to the national side. I watched the 'crème de la crème' play in the Scottish Reserve Tournament at Old Trafford Cricket Ground in Manchester. I was delighted to have managed to establish a nursery for the two Scottish senior sides. I really enjoyed working again with young people, especially because they brought such new and fresh ideas and approaches to the game.

To help others and spread knowledge about the new approaches to the game that I was introducing I put my ideas and their practical applications on paper. I wrote two books one in 1974 and 1977 – *Women's Hockey for the 70s* and *A Psychological Approach to the Women's Game*.

Chapter 22

*T*he late 1960s through the 70s was a time full of new challenge and not just on the hockey front. It began with a health problem. For some time I had an easily upset stomach and I wanted it put right. It was diagnosed as a gall bladder problem and the gall bladder needed to be removed.

The day I was admitted to the Convent Hospital in Edinburgh was a beautiful warm day. I was welcomed by the kindest staff of nuns. So much so that when I came round from the anaesthetic my first words were "when are you doing the operation?"The recovery was uncomplicated and for the two weeks following the operation I recuperated there. I was discharged then and ready to accept the next challenge.

Driven on by my interest in helping to improve the quality of life for individuals within families which began through my work with Barnardo's, I couldn't resist applying to an advertisement seeking people to come forward for the selection process to become a Marriage Guidance Counsellor. I was selected and went to Dundee University to undertake their training course. It was the mid 60s when I joined twelve others in one of the University's residences. The course was a residential course and started on a Friday and didn't finish till Monday afternoon

It was a thorough, demanding course that equipped its participants with a very clear idea of what Counsellors could do and how they were expected to behave.

The principles of Counselling were well explained. I became a qualified Marriage Guidance Counsellor and discovered a new world. Not only did I become a founder member of the Fife Marriage Guidance team but I met a new group of people with similar outlooks and interests. Beginning at the first selection weekend I found two particularly good new friends who also had children of similar age to mine. Margaret and Eira remained close friends until in the late 1990s when their circumstances changed and they were unable to remain in contact. Of course the additional knowledge gained in psychology gave me an in-depth and greater understanding of human behaviour.

The 1960s and 1970s witnessed a huge development in the new application of psychological approaches to improving all kinds of social, health and sporting concerns including hockey coaching. Demand for trained Counsellors was increasing. Even the Courts of Law were changing to become more open and more anxious to help children improve their behaviour instead of merely punishing them.

This change of attitude attracted me and I began to study how it was being put into practice. In Scotland a new Court, The Children's Panel, was being set up in each area of the community.

I was invited to become one of four volunteer Panellists and I was appointed the Vice-Chair of Fife Children's Panel. It was an exciting appointment. The Panels all over Scotland were feeling their way towards a family solution to prevent offending and re-offending. A

Reporter was appointed to each panel to provide formal legal advice and to ensure that the panellists kept within the bounds of current legislation. The Chair and Vice-Chair controlled the meetings with the children and their parents or guardians. Everyone had their say and then the conclusions were drawn up. An appropriate summary was made by the Chairman with the waiting child being informed of his or her fate. The decision of the Panel and reasons for the decisions and actions required were always made in front of the child and his/her supporters. This was a very new approach to make public, information which had previously taken place behind closed doors. It could be a hard thing for the Panellists to do but it did help to promote joint responsibility for the child's improved behaviour.

However, the options for action open to the panel were not extensive. Very often the most usual outcome was to have the child removed from the family to undertake a programme of reform for a set period usually in what was known as a List D Home. Panel members paid visits to these Homes on a regular basis to review the programmes of activity and the progress of children under their care.

I found the pioneering spirit of the whole introduction of these new programmes stimulating. The idea of a new concept backed by action meant taking some risks. Mistakes were made, inevitably, but to be part of the first wave of establishing new methods to try to help children and families have a better quality of life was a privilege.

Children were at the centre of mine and Douglas' lives and the importance of family life outweighed all other considerations.

During the 1960s and 1970s there were Christmases when the extended family gathered. The numbers at these events began to dwindle and we missed my uncles and aunts. We all missed our lovely New Year's Day with Auntie Nan who had moved from Dunard, Bathgate to a flat in St John's Road, Corstorphine.

We had lunch at the Zoo where she was a member. We all 'dressed' for it; the boys looked so good in their jackets and kilts and I fully admit to dressing them in kilts as often as I could.

Tea at Auntie Nan's afterwards was a scrumptious affair with all the best china being used! Replete and content we were ready for the journey home via car ferry at South Queensferry. Only once did the weather prevent us from using the ferry and we had to go the long way home over Kincardine Bridge.

Little did I know then how much ferries were to feature in my life later on.

The immediate difference made by the Forth road bridge when it was opened in 1964 was enormous. It meant we no longer had to wait in a long queue, not even to get through the toll booth! We were keen to be at the official opening of the Forth Bridge and my friends, the Thomsons, Sheila (from Bedford College) with Jane, Jono and Mary joined Jaffrey, Shona, Gavin and I to witnesses the ceremony at the North Queensferry end. Then walked upon it amongst the first pedestrians to use this magnificent piece of engineering. We all felt as if we had been taking part in a little bit of Scottish history.

The children were growing up and now getting into scrapes of their own. All five children were travelling by train to Edinburgh to school, on the 8.02am every morning. This meant an early start for everyone. On the train the younger children were supposedly being looked after by older members of the group. However, children will be children and there was some fun to be had.

In the early days the trains only had single carriages with a door on either side and no corridor. These were difficult for the guards to supervise. As the old trains were replaced with open carriage diesel trains bad behaviour reduced because all the children could be seen by all the travelling adults all the time.

There was, however, an incident with Lindsay's brand new waterproof. During a summer holiday he had grown to such a height he needed a new coat. The 'old' one was handed down to Jaffrey and probably again to Gavin although by the time he required one it was so well worn by the other two that he got a new one too!

In the case of Lindsay's new waterproof he left it by his seat in the compartment when he got out. Lindsay arrived home to report his sin and was promptly sent back to travel along the east coast railway line to Kirkcaldy to retrieve it.

Sally's biggest sin was to fool the staff at school by misleading them, in other words 'fibbing'. She used her appointments at the Dental Hospital in Chamber Street to her own advantage. She would write herself an appointment at the specified time, usually from lunchtime and later. Then she would present this to the teacher in charge. The staff were accustomed to receiving such letters and merely nodded permission for Sally to leave the school. Then Sally, finishing early, went to the Chambers Street Museum opposite the Dental Hospital and enjoyed her escape from school until it was time to get the train home.

I have only learnt lately of things that took place on the journeys to and from the school. It was a case of where ignorance is bliss!

Once the children were all either at school or at university, Sally at the University of Stirling, Lindsay at the University of Robert Gordon in Aberdeen, I discovered I had more time for other activities. There was also the bonus of another baby to enjoy. Grant was born to my brother Drew's first wife Mary Clegg.

As a child, Grant was often in my care. The two of us had a great affinity beginning from before he took his first steps to fetching and carrying him to primary school and then to Stewarts Melville. Grant thrived in the school atmosphere and he now has a successful career in finance. He and I continue to have a special relationship and to support each other when in need.

Chapter 23

*E*arly in 1972 a significant letter arrived. It was a letter headed Dunfermline College of Physical Education, Barnton, Edinburgh and was signed Mollie Abbott, Principal. It was a request inviting me to a meeting with her to discuss the possibility of a job on the College staff. This job would be something completely new. Title: Student Counsellor, the first College in Scotland to appoint one.

I was delighted at the idea and both Mum and Douglas were keen for me to pursue it. I reviewed my qualifications and experience:

1. Qualified PE Teacher – Bedford College.
2. Two years teaching at St Leonard's School.
3. Two years on the staff at Dunfermline College of Hygiene and Physical Education.
4. Qualified Marriage Guidance Counsellor.
5. Vice-Chair Children's Panel – Fife.

My qualifications and experience seemed to match the requirements.

During the years when the children were young I had, from time to time, filled in gaps in various schools including meeting Betty Spowart's need for extra staff at Woodmill School in Dunfermline. The other school that called frequently on my services was Mary Erskine Girls' School in Edinburgh.

When Mollie Abbott's letter came I had already agreed to teaching at the new schools amalgamation, Stewart's with Melville College for Boys. Therefore, I was not free until that contract was completed.

In spite of my other commitments I found it impossible to reject the offer from the College. I thought it was a wonderful opportunity. It contained everything I could have wished for. My Marriage Guidance training, my interest in applied psychology, my ability to work with young people in a sporting setting all contributed to my confidence in being able to accept the post. I went on to hold this post for nearly twenty years.

This post and that of international Scottish coach came at the same time. As a result, I had to resign from my school jobs.

The post of College Counsellor was not easy to fulfil as I discovered. The benefit of counselling was not necessarily appreciated by all members of staff although some supported it. It was also quite hard to convince some of the students of its value. To many staff and students, this stranger in their ranks had to be trusted with confidential personal information and this raised much suspicion. How could just talking resolve problems?

It did help that I was also PE trained and connected with hockey and having been a College Lecturer I also understood the pressures of college life. It is funny how one thing leads to another.

I enjoyed my years on the College staff, as much for all the talented, kind people I met as for the personal issues which students brought to me. There was one major person who made a huge contribution to me in particular and the Weir family as a whole.

I was keen to learn as much as I could about the skills and qualifications of counselling. To this end I applied for a place at a Conference on Counselling at Lancaster University.

I stayed in one of the resident's flats for the three-night length of the Conference. As the normal practice at such gatherings, many of the sessions were through group discussions so the members of the groups got to know each other.

I knew no-one but was glad to get to know the members of my group. One of these members was a lady called Joy Tiley. She was a principal lecturer in Education at Coventry College of Education. She and I became good friends right away. It transpired that she had not long returned from a year in Australia. Her mother had just died and she did not know anyone either.

That was the start of a very special friendship. Joy adopted the Weirs, who had no Aunts of their own. In the beginning Joy became my main academic advisor, especially in explaining how statistics work!

She continued to be closely involved as she and her father moved to Comrie, Perthshire when she took early retirement. After her father died she moved to a bungalow in Scone, by Perth. There she continues to enjoy an organised, quiet retirement and continues to be involved with the whole family, being godmother to one of the next generation too.

Mollie Abbott was a perceptive, intelligent, well respected and popular Principal. She was also a very good friend to me beyond the college walls. How she obtained her in-depth knowledge of her staff

I knew not, but she had it, in detail! For example, she knew that I liked to write.

How true! Ever since the day Auntie Nan discovered me, aged seven or eight, copying out parts of *'Black Beauty'* (Anna Sewell) on the dining room table, the urge to write has always remained strong. Although not always published there are still five unpublished novels sitting waiting on a shelf in my study!

This knowledge prompted Mollie to have 'one of her talks' with her Student Counsellor. Completely unexpectedly in that conversation she asked, "How would you like to take an M Phil degree?" The idea hit its target.

Would I like to do what? Without a second's hesitation the answer was emphatically yes. You bet! But it was to be a non-taught course with a thesis on a researched topic.

With Joy's help I was able to move into a wider network of educationalists. They allowed me to benefit from their experience and as a result I was able to meet up with a person who was willing to become my tutor.

Lady Venables, a senior lecturer at Birmingham University, agreed to guide me through the jungle of the requirements of submitting the necessary standard, style, content and analysis to achieve a successful thesis and obtain my Masters degree.

Statistics did not come easily for me, much too mathematical!! However, with a push here and a little explanation there from my friends I made the correct analysis and presentation.

The degree of M Phil was mine in 1980. The interview by two Professors, one from the University of St Andrews, the other from the University of Warwick, did not hold back on the difficulty of their questions. I still have no idea of the correct answer to the final one thrown at me by one of the Professors! She was knife sharp! But all was well and all the hard work mainly working on my own paid off. I have been ever grateful though for the generous availability of help from both Joy and Lady Venables.

The demands of a master's degree introduced me to a completely new way of study and outcome. No longer was the conclusion study for a set of written exams. Setting up, conducting research, developing valid surveys and writing the analysis in a thesis needed the application of a rigour and set of unique techniques that were also entirely different to those needed to produce short stories. There were also no absolute 'right' answers as there had been when studying the sciences

I enjoyed the rigour of academic research and quite unexpectedly was given the opportunity to go further.

Again, it began in College. Another beautiful spring day, getting warm, windless, the heavens were kind, blue with white clouds.

I had driven early to Cramond from College. I walked down to where the River Almond joins the attractive white inlet that joins the river Forth. As I stood there watching the activities of the members of the Cramond Yacht Club I noticed some movements on the opposite bank. A pathway on the other bank led to a small pier beside where I was standing. Waiting at the pier was a small, old fashioned rowing boat. It may have been old but it was well-shaped and solid. The boat held two passengers. A man was wielding a pair of oars. A ferryman!

The journey was short but indeed with no bridge how could anyone have crossed the water without a ferry?

The question buzzed round my head. I was intrigued so I set out to find the history of the Cramond ferry.

I quickly discovered there was little reference to it. I thought this was a strange omission as the crossing must have been well used for centuries to gain access to Dalmeny House.

I decided to investigate further. Where better to start than the Scottish Studies Department in the University of Edinburgh? I made an appointment with the Professor of History. I was sitting opposite him discussing the lack of information regarding ferries in Scotland and the fact that there seemed to have been little research had been carried out on this topic.

The Professor was immediately enthusiastically interested. "You would be better to consult Professor Geoffrey Barrow of the School for Scottish Studies. I'm sure he will take you on board. I'll ask him to see you right away."

He lifted the phone; Professor Barrow was free. It was incredible how smoothly everything was falling into place. There was the same response from Professor Barrow, only he added another dimension. "How would you like to do a PhD degree?" Hence the attempt to undertake a PhD was born. The Professor put his papers to one side, looked at his watch and spoke. "How about it?" he asked casually. It was 1986.

An animated discussion, a proposal and an acceptance, and I stood waiting for a bus in Chamber Street. I'm sure I was suffering from shock as I tried to get my head round the ideas of undertaking a PhD in Scottish History with the subject to be 'Communication in 19th Century Scotland with small ferries of particular interest'.

Let the research begin!

It was a task that took me, and usually a companion, most often Douglas or Joy, on a fascinating journey stretching from the South of Scotland, in Dumfriesshire, to both the east and west coasts including all the islands, , that dominated travel on the west coast. It involved specialist archivists and librarians and local historians. All were interested and very willing to help as much as they could. New material jumped into view.

My knowledge and the paper pile containing the research began to grow quite rapidly (personal computers were not widely available then).

Next came the writing up. There was an expectation that the work would be presented after approximately thirty six months or longer. I completed my thesis in just over thirty months. The final stage was an interview with two professors, both historians. It was a very different affair to my M.Phil grilling.

I was welcomed into the room with a most reassuring greeting.

One of the professors stood up, held out his hand and grinned at me. "Relax," he said. "This is a most interesting study. We look forward to a discussion about it. And, by the way your PhD is already yours. You have passed with room to spare. So relax!"

How could I relax after being given such news? I could not wait for my interview to be finished so that I could go and tell the family. Dr Marie Weir sounded quite good!!

It looked even better on the cover of the book that I wrote. Which was published in 1988 – *'Ferries in Scotland'*. Invitations to give talks to history societies followed.

But as time passed other matters could not be put to one side. The family's needs were changing. It was time to pay attention.

Chapter 24

*T*he 1980s and 1990s marked turning points for all the family. For the younger generation the excitement of adulthood and for Douglas and I plans for retirement, new interests and taking care of a few health and care difficulties.

The children were all grown up and in careers of their own: Sally in the Careers Service and Lindsay starting in a Building Society then moving to Recruitment Consultancy. Shona was in Aberdeen, moving on into a managerial course with WH Smith. Jaffrey was on a sales course with SAI and Gavin was starting out in a retail sports outlet with a Scottish entrepreneur. They were all learning, earning and gaining experience.

Our plans for retirement centred on downsizing. During the 1960s Douglas had had a heart attack one night as we walked home from watching Dunfermline Athletic Football team at Eastend Park. He was seen by a consultant in Edinburgh who confirmed that he required surgery and in 1984 he had a triple heart bypass operation. He was very brave about it and he made a very good recovery but the whole episode left me very nervous about the activities he should undertake. He had a little white pill to take before he did something strenuous. When I saw him swallow that I became anxious. As a result we stopped going dancing together and avoided potentially stressful events.

I'm sure that I was probably over anxious. Douglas was willing to try to do what he wanted to do but duly took care to save me from worrying.

As we planned for retirement Douglas was keen to keep in touch with the surgery but not work full time. A decision was made to sell Park Avenue house but retain the surgery and live in the cottage.

With this idea in mind the cottage required to be brought up to date. There was plenty of room to re-shape the cottage and Douglas knew a good builder. The changes that were made added significantly to the value and attractiveness of the whole house. A special feature was the conversion of the adjacent byre into a large lounge facing the magnificent view.

Two more bedrooms and a big conservatory addition made the whole cottage a great property. The timing of the move out of Park Avenue happened very suddenly when one day a man arrived at the front door of Park Avenue. He came with an offer to buy the house at a set price. Douglas agreed to the price and was seduced by the fact that all the paperwork was so straight forward. The transaction took no time at all and we rushed into a move to the cottage. Idyllic though the cottage was it proved not to be a suitable retirement house. It was very isolated and was not an easy commute to work for anyone. We united to look for a more suitable house and sell the cottage. We found our perfect compromise at Gowkhall, on the outskirts of Dunfermline on the road to the Kincardine Bridge.

This was a modern four bedroomed modern house with an interesting demi-floor providing a balcony overlooking a large lounge. A spiral wooden stair connected the two and provided a major feature to the room. The garden was not too big to manage but there was plenty of room for the visiting family plus two cocker spaniel dogs. The house and its location provided the best of both worlds: a little bit of country and good access to town.

It was from this house that the first wedding took place. In 1989 Lindsay took Mhairi Helen Luke, nursing specialising in Health Visiting, as his wife. They went to Glasgow to live. It was not long before Morven was born and in a further fourteen months her sister Kirsten was born.

These two beautiful babies, together with Mhairi's ability to share them, immediately extended my range of activities. It was easy for me to drive from Gowkhall to Glasgow. I just loved looking after the children and the months flew past. Of course I was still continuing in my post as Student Counsellor at Dunfermline College.

The family continued to grow and in 1990 Jaffrey married Kathleen Mary Kelly, a nurse specialising in midwifery. They moved close by to Kinross and their eldest daughter, Johanna, was very soon born, followed by Douglas and then Jennifer.

Kathleen's parents, Rev. Clifford and Johanne Kelly, on retirement also chose, first of all a house in Scotlandwell and secondly in Kinross.

Mhairi then added to their two with Caroline arriving before they left Glasgow and Robert completing to their number after they came to live in Dunfermline. To have all seven grandchildren within such easy reach was a huge bonus.

My grandchildren and their development and interests, successes and failures bolstered my strength to tackle the ups and downs of changing care demands. Both Mum and Douglas had reached an age and stage when the impact of health problems could no longer be ignored.

Mum was beginning to need more help with everyday things and her house was becoming too much for her to handle. Together we began to explore what arrangements might be possible. Mum was very keen to remain as independent as possible. Sheltered Housing seemed to be the answer. The nearest sheltered housing scheme was an apartment in Stockbridge, Edinburgh. These were brand new retirement apartments and Do became a first buyer and secured a ground floor, two bedroomed flat with a nice lounge, good access to buses on the road directly outside and a Tesco opposite. It was as good as it was possible to find. Daily visits were possible because Carlisle Court was close to my work at Dunfermline College.

This move was made easier because Mum herself made no difficult refusals. She did not want to move from her bungalow in Dunfermline but she accepted what seemed to be inevitable without a fuss.

The other comforting benefit was that Drew's first wife, Mary, lived in a flat about three hundred yards along the road in Stockbridge. She called on Mum regularly but Mum too made her own life.

When she first moved into Carlisle Court she still drove the car. However, one day I was called to Ravelston Dykes where the inevitable had happened. Mum had pulled out at a T junction into the path of a car travelling straight along the main road. There was a bump. No-one was hurt but the cars were damaged. That was the end of Mum's driving. She used the bus instead!

She went outside to the bus stop. In spite of failing eyesight she caught the first bus that came along. One day she found herself in Joppa! She mostly found her way to the restaurants of Wilkies, Jenners and Binns where the waitresses got to know her and buttered her roll and helped her with her soup.

How she crossed all these broad, busy roads goodness knows. Mum said she just asked the nearest person to help guide her. She always got help and made friends along the way.

As Mum progressed into her late 80s she continued to appear to be well although she was diagnosed with a type of lymphoma. The consultant at the Great Western was exactly right for her. He sized her up so accurately and treated her accordingly with no severe medication.

To everyone's relief Mum made a full recovery. She just loved to be told she did not look her age and neither did she.

Mum remained remarkably well and active and we were able to go away on holiday for short breaks, often to North Berwick.

One weekend this was arranged with the first night being spent at Gowkhall. However, when I went into her room in the morning she was not at all well and she was taken immediately to hospital in Dunfermline. She was very ill but gradually she recovered again. Her stamina was amazing. However, it became clear that she could no longer live alone.

Luckily a solution presented itself. Bandrum Nursing Home, a newly built home on the road from Gowkhall to Saline, had just opened..

This was a perfect arrangement able to provide the everyday care that Mum now needed and accessible for the family, being only minutes away in the car. Mum had lots of visitors and always liked to look her best. She was stylish. Her taste was impeccable and she had a great eye for what suited her best. Mum always looked smartly dressed, colour co-ordinated in all the blues and purples which were her favourite colours.

Mum made a huge effort to look her best and even into her nineties enjoyed the compliments that resulted.

Douglas and I settled into a new rhythm of life, spending more time with Mum and our new grandchildren. After much thought we decided on one further house move and started looking for a bungalow.

Douglas spotted a house in Kinross even before it was notified as being for sale. It was ideally placed with a magnificent view at the back overlooking the long pastoral stretch to the bottom of the Ochil Hills. It was a four bedroomed bungalow standing in the midst of a good sized garden. There was a large lounge, a neat sitting room, three bedrooms with the fourth to convert into a most necessary study for me. The move from Gowkhall to Kinross was booked to take place in July 1992.

It was a beautiful hot summer's day and Sally and I went to Bandrum early in the morning prior to collecting a lawn mower from Inverkeithing. Mum was very frail and not keen to chat with us.. I saw the doctor who reassured me that my mother was just tired. In the half-hour it took us to collect the lawnmower Mum died. Life changed for me and it would never be the same again. Mum had been a mainstay in encouraging and supporting me to strive to achieve my potential and I still miss her very much.

Kinross really did become a new start for us and despite our sad beginning we had much to keep us actively engaged in the future.

"How would you like to become a grandmother again?" Kathleen and Mhairi both asked me. Well there was only one answer to that and first Johanna and then Kirsten joined the clan.

The next 'batch' arrived on cue. I was delighted. I added Grandmother to mother and mother-in-law to my list headed 'must learn more'.

Still more babies arrived. A boy had not yet appeared. And surely one did. Douglas Clifford Kelly was a gift Jaffrey and Kathleen welcomed. He was a sturdy little fellow with a mop of thick, curly hair and an even temperament and named after his two grandfathers.

Not long after our move to Kinross we had a lovely opportunity. Jaffrey, Kathleen, Johanna and little Douglas came to stay with us for a few months whilst they built their own house in Kinross. It was a great opportunity to get to know our grandchildren really well. My Douglas loved it. He had time to spend with the grandchildren that he had not had with his own children. It was a pleasure to watch them all together.

The early 1990s kept changes coming to impact on my life.

In the west of Scotland two events of great significance took place, in the same hospital. One was a birth and the second was a death.

Mhairi gave birth to her third baby, Caroline, in the Royal Alexandra Hospital in Paisley. She was a lovely baby, good weight, dark hair, deep brown eyes and smiling. Who would have thought that such a wee scrap would become an international footballer at the age of 17?

She was brought back to their new house in a move to Dunfermline. I stayed in Glasgow to look after Morven and Kirsten while Mhairi was in hospital.

At the same time and in the same hospital my eldest cousin Dr Inglis Walker was admitted so I was able to visit regularly and memories came flooding back.

Inglis was the eldest son of James Walker, Mum's eldest brother who was the managing director of Walker & Sons in Bathgate and latterly a County Councillor on his retirement to Kilmacolm.

Inglis was clever. He was dux of George Watson's Boys School in Edinburgh. He trained as a doctor at the University of Edinburgh and served in the Royal Navy in the Far East during the war. He was appointed as Principal Consultant in charge of Hairmyres Hospital, the specialist hospital for patients suffering from tuberculosis, until it closed and then he became an assessor of patients suffering from asbestos poisoning.

Inglis was a gentle soul and he grew up to be a good doctor who was well respected by his staff.

When we were children Inglis had seemed a bit remote to me being some ten years my senior and I had more contact but not more in common with his sister Margaret. I came from a sports minded background whereas Margaret did not know what the word 'sport' meant!

Margaret was an admirable, conscientious person whose great love was home economics. She trained at the Atholl Crescent School of Home Economics in Edinburgh and became a teacher and eventually Head of the Home Economics Department in St Columba's School for Girls in Kilmacolm.

Neither Inglis nor Margaret married and they lived with and looked after Nora and James, their parents. On the death of their parents they bought a house together and settled down to a measured life of service to others with the occasional foray into Europe on a cruise or a week's stay in some interesting place in Scotland or Europe.

As the Weirs had a set pattern of going to Arran for our summer holidays it was easy to pay a visit annually to see Margaret and Inglis in Kilmacolm. They welcomed the family with open arms and a lovely tea.

Margaret and Inglis epitomised the Walker family principles of service, caring for others and generosity. These values can be traced down the family tree and I hope that they are implanted strongly in the rising generation.

Other than Jaffrey, Inglis was the first of my Bathgate cousins to die and this marked a turning point for my own generation and during the next decade Margaret, Mary and Drew were lost to the family.

Chapter 25

Some may have thought our choice of holiday restricted, even limited. It probably was but it did not seem so at the time. To go to Arran year after year was always anticipated with high hopes and expectations.

But it was Joy's influence that took me on holidays that I otherwise would never have enjoyed.

The two of us went on short breaks to Innsbruck in Austria, Annecy in France, Lucerne, Switzerland and endlessly to Keswick in the Lake District. Joy was an experienced traveller while I dragged my feet at the thought of going on holiday. I was content to visit different parts of Scotland and Douglas' only holiday love was Arran! That was travel enough for him. Not surprising after six years in military service in Burma and the Himalayas in the Second World War. Mum and I went for a summer break every year and were content to visit Scotland's erstwhile holiday resorts such as North Berwick, the Marine Hotel or, further afield, to Gatehouse-of-Fleet, the Calais Palace Hotel.

Douglas and I settled well into life in Kinross. Whilst I continued to study and write Douglas joined the Bowling and Probus Clubs. However, he began to feel unwell around the Xmas of 1995 and it became obvious that he must see a consultant again to get a further diagnosis.

Douglas was sent to the City Hospital in Edinburgh where he was diagnosed with a disease of the Lupus family. There was neither known cure nor indeed treatment. Douglas was transferred to the rheumatic ward of the Western General Hospital in Edinburgh.

Over a period of nearly three months he gradually grew weaker. The doctor in charge knew very little about Douglas' disease and the consultant was difficult to pin down for discussion so it took a while for us all to come terms with the fact that Douglas was dying. It was an unhappy and anxious time but Douglas remained cheerful and stoical throughout.

Douglas died quietly and peacefully in March 1996 with the family all round him. It was a sad day. What would I do without him? He was my stay and rock and we had been very happy together. Neither of us was perfect but we complemented each other very well especially when major decisions needed to be made. We all still miss him very much.

The second half of the 1990s had yet more surprises for me and this time of a very happy nature.

There were two more babies on the way; one baby in each family.

In Dunfermline it was a boy. Robert quickly learnt how to more than hold his own in a houseful of girls. His counter cousin in Jaffrey's family was a girl, Jennifer, and she too stole the hearts of her siblings.

I also had another surprise. Gavin married Deborah Fahey in her local church followed by a full family and friends reception at Haigh Hall in Aspull.

The incoming new century swept in a trail of personal situations that required a different set of skills,

Up until now I had considered myself to be fit. I expected to be able to do all the things I had always done without question. I discounted a bit of high blood pressure and the removal of my gall bladder as just minor issues. I was well and still playing golf on holiday and walking and cycling regularly.

However, one morning early in 2004, as was my wont, I was walking round all the windows and drawing back the curtains. I bent down to turn on the radiator in one of the bedrooms. I found I could not straighten up and was enduring a searing pain in my back.

This turned out to be due to a disintegration of three vertebrae in my back, two cervical and one lumbar. They had simply given way and broken up. It was Osteoporosis!

Hospitalisation was the first step. Followed by much and a slow build up of exercise. It took six weeks before I was discharged from hospital and a further six months after that for the vertebrae to heal. The greatest help was a comment from my long-standing Bedford College friend Chris. She had had a similar attack and she assured me: "It will get better". And it did.

Nevertheless, this changed my focus and once recovered I began to spend much more time with my grandchildren, picking them up from school and going to support them in all sorts of activities including football, badminton, swimming and debating events.

In Dunfermline I clocked up forty school assemblies and I enjoyed every minute.

There was more time for friends too and mine stretched across the generations from my own school and student days through hockey and counselling to work and writing times. I have never been without people to meet up with but it has taken time to get used to living for the first time on my own.

The new century has brought yet more wonderful surprises. Grant married Elizabeth Langley and they had Harry and Archie, some 10 years younger than their Weir second cousins.

Then in 2007 after nearly seven years of marriage Deborah announced that she was pregnant. What excitement and pleasure Jessica has brought to us.

As I look forward to my next challenges, many appear to be of a technical nature, advances in technology have already helped me a lot. The quality and size of hearing aids for example just amaze me.

Who would have thought too that from the black and white screen viewed for the first time on Coronation Day that television could be in colour, far less having multiple channels and programmes to choose from each night or watched on a tiny hand held device?

Staying in touch is also so much quicker. Mobile phones, texting, email and other new communication pathways mean I can access the world from my living room. Hearing from a granddaughter in Malawi about her sister's British based exam results was almost as unbelievable as seeing her on SKYPE.

Jessica, now aged seven, uses computer technology the way I used pen and paper. I wish that I could be here to see what technology Jessica will consider ordinary when she reaches my age or beyond.

The technology I could do with now has also just been invented. The driverless car! That would suit me perfectly because I could once again have independent means of travel lost to permanent damage to my eyesight as a result of a stroke in 2013.

I have revelled in every one of my roles especially the intricacies of managing to be the best wife, mother, mother-in-law and grandmother that I could be. I have been so lucky that each of my daughters-in-law have been so willing to befriend me too.

Despite being unable to read back to myself this book that I have written in longhand I have also once more found that the drive to write is as strong as ever and there may yet be another chapter to write!

I am now nearly the last one standing in my generation as my mother was for hers.

I have been so lucky to have had an active, incredibly happy life.

This story is of course not yet finished. There is such hope for the future as my grandchildren take to the stage of adulthood. They are confident, capable people with a great capacity for love and I feel very privileged to be included by them into their circles. I look forward to their adventures.

My memoir is dedicated to my eight grandchildren, five children, my daughters-in-law and my nephew, his wife and two children.

There is time for much more in your life than you think possible and when one door shuts another door really does open. Just embrace it!

THE END

Wedding, 1951

Whitingbay, 1968

*Marie first Scottish National Coach with the goal scorer Marietta
Craigie, Wembley, 1972, Scotland 2 England 0*

PhD, 1986

40th Wedding Anniversary, 17 August 1991

Skiddaw with Dean and Roan, 2000

Marie and grandchildren, 2014

Lightning Source UK Ltd
Milton Keynes UK
UKOW06f0223270516

275093UK00017B/520/P